I0505802

Confessions of a London Boulevardier

Excerpts from an Artist's (so-called) Life

Francis Charlton

Vol.1
Stroll On
2nd Edition

Confessions of a London Boulevardier

Excerpts from an Artist's (so-called) Life

Francis Charlton

Vol.1
Stroll On
2nd Edition

for
Eloise
my inspiration

All characters and events portrayed in this story are fictitious.
Any similarity to actual events or persons living, dead or undead, unless used for
satirical purposes is purely coincidental.

Excerpts from an Artist's (so-called) life...

Are mobile phones the new passive smoking?

Walking into a department store, a mock Glock holstered under my jacket, I approached the customer services desk. 'Excuse me,' I said, 'do you work here?' I'd noticed that criminally insane sales assistants had replaced distinctly unhelpful staff.

'What's it got to do with you?'

'I have a query,' I said, avoiding eye contact, 'do you sell decaffeinated coffee tables?'

'How should I know? I'm only here to provide you with wrong information and drain your wallet. Take the elevator to the third floor and ask them yourself. Now fuck off before I call security!'

Taking the stairs to the 4th floor, I don't trust elevators and I always avoid going to where I'm directed, you need to know that sales assistants are from the Evening Standard vendors school of misdirection. Reaching the 4th floor, a department manager approaches me, all the while talking into his sleeve like a secret service agent or a deranged tailor. 'How can I help you?' He asks, looking at me and scratching his head.

I reach under my jacket and feel the warmth of the mock Glock.'I've come about the McJob advertised,' I lied.

'Do you want irregular fries with your burger?' he whispers into his sleeve.

I take this as an opportunity to leave, 'I have to go on a binge wank,' I say waving to him and stepping into the stairwell. Reaching the 5th floor I think, who do I tell that the CIA have a wiretap on my phone, because they believe I know the whereabouts of Elvis. And more importantly who would believe me. I sit at an empty table in the café.

'Who the fuck are you?' A waitress asks me, pen poised like she's going to stab me through the ear.

'Some people call me the space cowboy. Some call me the gangster of love.'

'I'll call you Maurice,' she says, 'now what the fuck do you want?'

'I want to go on the pull, neck a few WKDs, monster a kebab, and contract a STI.'

'I'll get you an Americano,' she says making a note on a pad. She tears it off and places it under a sugar bowl.

I discretely turn the note toward me to read what was on it. *'Meet me on the roof in 15 minutes,'* it said. Curious! I thought.

Listening to a group of jitterati drinking double espressos and talking bollocks, 'what we have here is an opportunity! I'm a public relations executive and believe me I'll tell you anything.'

I had an irrepressible urge to yawn.

'You're going to fucking kill yourself if you miss this opportunity,' the PR guy continued.

Me? I couldn't stop myself from yawning. I looked back at the sugar bowl, ten minutes to go. I pondered the question of sachets. Sugar; brown, white and sweetener, in packaging more suited to feminine hygiene products. There was a container of tomato sauce, brown sauce, salad cream, salt and pepper all in perfectly formed sachets.

It struck me like an epiphany, they were portion controlled! Just then a perfectly proportioned waitress appeared with an Americano, she like the accompaniments was portion controlled.

'Would you like a cake with that?' She queried, setting down the coffee. She was flaunting portion controlled products at me. I get up to leave.

'You haven't finished your coffee and there's still five minutes before your assignation. Candy hasn't started her break yet.'

Assignation! Candy! 'How do you know?' I ask staring at her breast where a badge says *'Hi. I'm Mandy.'*

'Know what?' She looks at me puzzled. A trickle of sweat meanders its way down my face. I drink the coffee in two slurps and walk quickly to the till.

'Hi. I'm Sandy, how would you like to pay?'

'Cash,' I say, placing a perfectly folded £5 note on the counter. 'Keep the change.'

'You'd better hurry or you'll be late for your tryst. Candy has other appointments.'

Does everyone know? I think and start to shake. Noticing a toilet sign I decide to wash my face.

'Have a nice day!' Sandy calls out, momentarily distracting me. PR guy takes the opportunity to hand me his business card.

'You never know?' He says. I glance at the card,

'GIVING IT LARGE'

it says, no name, no number.

I rush to the toilet and splash cold water over my face.

'Would sir like a sanity towel?' The toilet attendant looks at me in the mirror, looking at himself he smiles at his reflection, which doesn't smile back. 'I'm Randy. I'll be your toilet attendant today and believe me it's a pleasure. You wouldn't believe the riff-raff that come in here and engage me in conversation. 'Is this the toilet for the inane?' They say, looking at me, toilet plunger in hand, ready to er.., well, plunge. Actually that's not wholly true, although the plunger bit is. My plunger is less a tool more a purifier for the Lord. Often, as I try to suck someone's brain out through their nose, the Lord whispers in my ear that we are instruments to the one true path, my plunger and me. Many times, as I've stalked commuters on the Underground or hidden from the police behind privet hedges, I've questioned my faith. BUT the LORD always whispers in my ears, in stereo I might add: 'PLUNGE THEM RANDY! PLUNGE THEM!' And I know I must continue his work.'

Shuddering I make my way around Randy, who is idly toying with his plunger and winking at his reflection in the taps. 'I've got to get the fuck out of here.' I think.

Randy calls out as I push through the doors. 'You've only got a minute. Candy won't wait!'

I follow the signs to a bank of elevators and with only my ego for company enter the first empty one.

'Going up,' the disembodied computer voice says as the doors close.

Why did I do it? I hate elevators with their low hum of muzak and the monotone voice informing you what floor comes next, and 'stand clear of the doors,' and, 'doors closing.'

4

'Ladies and gentlemen. A good service is operating on London Underground this afternoon.'

'Fuck me, this can't be right!' I say out loud.

'Stand well clear, vehicle reversing.'

'Do me a favour,' I think, moving towards the doors to get out.

'Insert your ticket into the...'

'Shut the fuck up! I scream trying to pry apart the closed doors.

'Just what do you think you're doing Dave?'

For fuck's sake how does it know my name? I get two fingers between the doors and start to pull.

'Dave, I really think I'm entitled to an answer to that question.'

I get two more fingers in the crack.

'Dave!'

'Fuck you!' I shout. Why does this fucker of an elevator sound like HAL, I think as the doors open. Rushing into the corridor I notice a sign indicating an entrance to the roof garden. I open a glass door and step onto path. As the door automatically closes behind me I can just make out faint strains of muzak, *'Daisy, Daisy.'* The sound is quickly cut off, as the door clicks shut, to be replaced by birdsong. I notice under some trees, in the centre of the garden tables and chairs, and follow the path towards them. A candle is burning on a table with a square of paper slowly being engulfed by melting wax, on it is written, 'You're late, Candy.' It was obviously a past-it note.

But. What. Does. It. Mean?

That I'm late for our meeting? Or that she's the late Candy? I narrow my eyes and finger my Glock, is this a murder that needs solving or a question of semantics? Suddenly a wind blows the candle out and from a bamboo arrangement a geezer steps out.

5

'Hi, I'm Andy, he says, moving his hand to inside his cream Aquascutum double-breasted trench coat.

'I wouldn't do that,' I say, mirroring his movements.

'Okay,' he says, 'let me give you my business card,' gesturing to an inside pocket.

'Okay, but use two fingers and take it out slowly.' He hands me the card, printed on it, in letters slightly raised it says:

**You'll receive a free Parker Pen
just for inquiring.**

'I don't want a Parker Pen and I don't want information, so get fucked.' I turn and make my way to the glass doors. Throwing them open and stepping into a reception area, I find myself, once again, at the customer service desk.

'How may I misdirect you?' An assistant asks me and while I ponder a response she places a sign on the desk which reads:

WE ARE GO FOR LAUNCH.

From out of, fuck knows where, two rentasecurity approach me. 'Excuse me Sir,' one of them sneers at me, 'we've had complaints that you are wandering around the store not buying anything. We are, therefore, obliged to ask you to leave.'

I pull out my Glock and point it at them. 'If you want to avoid the BANG! And the searing pain and the back of your head flying into the wall behind you and the brain splatter decorating the wall like a bad Jackson Pollack painting, then I would step out of my way.' I eye a way out and follow it to its conclusion. I hail a black cab, and as it pulls into the traffic I look out of the rear view window at the security goons, who are now weeping on each other's shoulder.

Excerpts from an Artist's (so-called) life...

Be afraid, be very afraid.

'Where to guvnor?' The driver was looking at me in his rear view mirror.

'Gallery X, tout de suite,' I say. Why I said that I don't fucking know.

'Tout de suite,' the cabbie mimics, 'tout de suite,' are you having a fucking laugh? Are you having a fucking laugh at my expense? Am I the subject of your fucking ridicule? Fuck me, you fucking cunt who the fuck do you think you are? I can't fucking believe it, you've got more front than Selfridge's. You get into my cab, ask me to take you to a fucking destination and expect me to get you there 'tout de suite,' you fucking cunt. What do you think I am, a fucking cab for hire, if you wanted one of them you should have got a mini-cab innit!' I had that Mervyn Shagg in the back of the cab the other day. 'Mervyn,' I said, 'where to?'
'Waterstones, I'm reading from my new novel,' he said through his nose. The fucker then started reading from a manuscript he had with him. After ten minutes I thought, this fucker won't shut up. 'Mervyn,' I said, 'enough innit, what you want to write about is real life.'

The stories I can tell you, my son. The people I've had in the back of my cab, the cyclists I've run over. These are stories from the street, I said, and would you Adam and Eve it, he jumped out at the next set of traffic lights. And he didn't leave a fucking tip.'

Liking the idea I took the opportunity to exit the taxi at a set of lights on Charing X Road. Throwing a fake £10 note through the window I shouted, 'ciao my son.' The cabbie looked at the £10 note, looked at me, looked for an audience and screamed, 'you call that a fucking tip?' Before cutting in front of a Mercedes with diplomatic plates, waving his fist and shouting out of his window,'I'd hang them! We won the war! And National Service didn't do no one no harm!'

Excerpts from an Artist's (so-called) life...

One size fits all

In all this excitement I'd forgotten where I was going. Noticing an Old Bill walking towards me, I said, 'excuse me I seem to be lost!'

Looking at me like I was an asylum seeker wanting directions to the benefits office, he leaned into my face, and unholstering a can of pepper spray said, 'would sir like to kettle?'

Stepping back I said, 'no fanx,' and, I can only say that I did my best to avoid a showdown, tried to enter a bookshop.

The Old Bill suddenly sprang into the doorway blocking it with his, not ungenerous bulk, 'is sir a bohemian? Is sir lost outside of Soho? Is sir perhaps louche?' And raising his pepper spray took aim.

Before I could attempt to outdraw him a group St. Martin's students pushed past him, their arms stuffed with stolen art books, being chased by an overweight security goon. The Old Bill seeing an opportunity gave chase, breaking pace only to pepper spray the security guard in the face and raise his finger to a group of Japanese tourists and shout, 'Met 1. Foyles 0,' before running in the opposite direction the students had come from.

Turning into Old Compton Street, I thought there's time for coffee and cake. Arriving at Patisserie Valerie, I seated myself at my usual upstairs table. With an hour to kill before the opening, time enough for four espresso doppios and a slice of black forest gateaux.

Clara came over, 'your usual,' she said, making a note. Why, I don't know, but decided not to ask remembering the situation at lunchtime.

'How's it going? Any parts?' I ask. Clara was an actor and the muse for L.F. She supplemented her income by waitressing and performing mime on the South Bank. Working in a restaurant I could understand, mime made my trigger finger itch.

'Yep! Possibly a crowd scene in Shakespeare's Shrew at the Globe.'

There was an obvious, and some may say pretentiously deafening, silence at the next table of resting actors, who begin making furtive notes on napkins. And then, losing their composure waved, called, beckoned and even pleaded for the bill.

As Clara prepared their bill I noticed D.F. at a corner table and tried to avoid his eye. Too fucking late. He showed his companions five fingers and walked over. 'Dave, how are you?' He faked interest, 'how's the work going for your show. Are you on top of it? If you don't want the space I'll take it off your hands.' And without waiting for a reply turned and walked back to his table. The fucker's a dial tone I thought.

As the table of actors took their leave, all wanting to get out and speed dial their agents, Clara bounded up. Tray of espressos and gateaux balanced on one hand, the other scooping up the tips from the actors' table.

'Tight bastards, they'll all be belling their agents and whining about getting them work at the Globe.'

'You did make it obvious.' I said obviously.

'Obviously I'm an actor, I'll make them believe anything they want to. In fact I've got a three month run in Kevin Spacey's new production at the Old Vic. Which reminds me how's your exhibition coming alone? Doesn't it open in a month? D.F. pricked up his ears. Taking a leaf out of Clara's book, I said, loudly and emphatically, 'only got to frame a few pieces and it's ready to hang.' In the corner D.F. made a call. Probably to the Samaritans.

Four double espressos later, and wiping a smidgen of cream off my knitted tie, I order an espresso to go. I'm feeling wired as Clara deposits the steaming fragrant papercup at my table. I hand her a folded £20 note saying, 'keep the change babe,' and ask her does she want to come as my plus-one to the Gallery X opening.

Pocketing the £20 note and shredding the bill she informs me that L.F. is taking her and if I see her there to ignore her. Back on Old Compton Street I'm momentarily perplexed. 'Do I,' I say to a passing tourist who, thinking I'm a street lunatic, turns and walks back the way he came, 'want to arrive at the cheesed-off and whining opening sober? Hell no!' I conclude out loud. And downing my coffee in the requisite two slurps' stride off towards the Groucho.

Excerpts from an Artist's (so-called) life...

Waiting for Godot

The call of the Evening Standard seller on the corner of Dean Street, *'Stanit! Stanit! Read all about it in the Stanit!'* Was, it must be said, and I say it with a straight face, music to my ears. In the confines of Soho I knew I was home. Not that I'd been home in the last five days. In turn sleeping on a bench in Soho Square, a bench in London Zoo, M's bed with M, G's bed with her boyfriend (any port in a storm, as they say), and a front garden in Holland Park. In the latter I acquired three garden gnomes which I sold at Camden Market and with the proceeds breakfasted on two pints of Guinness and a fry-up, and followed up with another pint of Guinness to wash it down.

Finding myself outside the Groucho, I think choices. Go in and talk bollocks whilst drinking copious amounts of alcohol or make my way to the opening via every pub, bar and off-license on the way. For five minutes I stand indecisively on the pavement, feeling a cliché moment slowly arrive like the dawn. I feel inside my crumpled linen jacket. Fondling two dice, I blow on them and throw them at the door of the Groucho. Evens, I go in. Odds, pub crawl.

Looking down I count two on one dice and two on the other. 'Four absinthes,' I order at the bar, 'and a pint of Guinness to help wash these dice down.' Swallowing the dice and draining the glass in one fluid movement, I spy through the foam at the bottom of the glass T. and V. in a corner, quite obviously slumming it.

Balancing two glasses of absinthe in each hand and ordering four more, I make my way over. 'Dave Hi,' says T. and from out if the corner of my eye I notice a movement. A steely eyed Ray Winstone lookalike stands in front of me and whispers, 'Hi my name's Roger and I believe you're packing.'

'He's a friend,' says T. Roger takes a beat, looks me in the eye, removes his hand from inside his coat and, barely audibly, says, 'Respect.'

I offer everyone an absinthe as four more are delivered. Taking the tray, I say to T. 'What's this about Bermondsey being the new West End?'

'It's all in the minds of the public relations executives, who're working for every business, start-up, collective and their High Street corporate master to make it so,' he sneers, 'it's time to burst the bubble.

'And tonight we are pricks!' says V.

'A new campaign?' I ask.

'We call it 'the Sincerely Jack initiative,' said T. 'We're going to stencil knives, axes and surgical instruments buried into PR designed copy and lots of red paint! Bermondsey the New West End-do me a fucking favour.' At that moment D.H., strolls over and places a hand on my shoulder.

Excerpts from an Artist's (so-called) life...

Based on actual events

'Still drinking?' D.H. says as I reach under my jacket. I notice Roger mirror my movements. Sensing a blip in the matrix and looking at his hand which is now holding a glass of absinthe D.H. shakes his head. 'Anyway,' he says, 'got everything ready for the exhibition?' and without waiting for a reply says, 'my new piece, which I'm calling *'Secular Ritualisms and Roadside Memorials the Aftermath of Death and the Introduction of Dead Flowers Symbolising the Finality of Existence,'* will be unveiled at my new studio in a converted crematorium in Catford tomorrow at 12noon precisely. Call my PR company and tell them to put you on the *'Invite Shite'* list.' And without waiting for a reply turns and walks into the toilet. There follows a strangled cry 'Arrrrh! My fucking hand.' And the sound of a body hitting the floor. Two cronies rush into the toilet and carry out an ashen faced D.H., drooling and singing, *'going to go to the spirit in the sky, that's where I'll go when I die, when I die and they lay me to rest, going to go to the place that's the best...'*

We all turn as the door opens and what only can be described as an undertaker points and curls his finger towards a waiting hearse with its engine idling at the kerb.

The cronies heave D.H. into the back seat and get in themselves, followed by the undertaker, who can be heard saying, as the door is closing, 'Catford RIP.'

Or at least that's what we think we heard him say.

Excerpts from an Artist's (so-called) life...

Life imitating Art

'Gotta go,' I say, 'gotta opening to invade.'
'You on the Gallery X list? Queries T.
'No fucking idea,' I say, 'it's a pop-up, open 72 hours and then it's 'Oh! Vienna.'
'I think you mean 'Goodnight Vienna,' T. corrects me.
'No, 'Oh! Vienna,' is a new 80s retro night at the old Raymond Review, playing New Romantic music with a disco beat.' I glance at my watch. Two minutes to nine, plenty of time. I shake hands with T. and V. 'Where's your mysterious friend?' I ask.
'Probably on his way to Heathrow. He's flying to Rome for a few days and staying in a hotel a few streets from where I was born,' says Vincenzo.
Stifling back a yawn, I pull on a pair of rubber gloves and enter the Soho night. T. and V. get onto a tandem and cycle off to a cry of 'Hi Ho Vincenzo!'
Checking the address and directions as I didn't know the alley where the gallery was situated even existed before today, I set off crossing into Meard Street in the direction of Poland Street. I find the the alley on the fourth attempt of retracing my steps around the block. A narrow cobbled short stretch of road, with no pavements, which was essentially the alley, led onto a small communal gardens with terraced properties surrounding it.

Gallery X was housed in what was a terraced Georgian house now converted in a white cube makeover. Opposite was a similar building, this one converted into tarts' flats with the requisite red light outside, shining like a beacon for the many lost and lonely up from the provinces for the day. Fifi, Cleo, Candy and Mistress Red all had their door bell panels lit up, and if it wasn't for the fact that I'd swallowed my dice, I'd probably have a 50/50 chance of spending the night with all four ladies of the night.

Instead I handed my invite to a security guard who scanned it with an infra-red device nodded to a guy at the rope who allowed me through and into the exhibition. Both of the security guards were dressed identically. From their wraparound shades to their black tee shirts, which curiously were printed with the word SECRETARY across the back. Now this was, let me tell you, a fucking big spelling error at the tee shirt printers, or was it? Was it deliberate, a play on words. Was it part of the Gallery X opening theatre? Why the fuck was I pondering this, I thought. I couldn't actually care less.

Passing through, what appeared to be a sphincter shaped doorway, I was handed a bottle of Becks and a shot glass of Nemiroff, a Ukraine vodka, by a hunchback dressed like an undertaker. 'My assistants will cater to all your needs for the rest of the evening,' he slurred before dragging himself over to J. and D. who were each holding a hand of K.M. K dressed like Shirley Temple was looking a little dazed.

'Hi Dave,' said J. 'How's the exhibition coming along?'
Avoiding the question I say, 'what's the matter with K?'
'Too much chicken,' says D.
'Right,' I say, 'thinking what the fuck's he talking about.'

Excerpts from an Artist's (so-called) life...

Are we having fun yet?

Suddenly six dwarfs blow a fanfare from miniature trumpets and in walks J.J., with a blonde on either arm. Me thinks I think J.J. is overcompensating. Coming over to me he says, 'Hello Clarice,' about turns and walks towards a side room. 'Don't forget,' he whispers, 'to invite me to your opening.' Passing J. and D., I hear him say, 'beware the moon, boys.'

D. bares his teeth and growls. The two blondes hold J.J. even tighter. 'Thanks,'he says as he disappears into the room which appears to be full of clouds.

I decide to follow him. Two security guys stop me. 'Off limits, enter any other room,' they say simultaneously. I notice these guys are wearing tee shirts which say SECRECY.

The gallery is filling up fast. But. Where the fuck is the art? A dwarf on stilts fills my glass with more vodka and hands me another beer. 'Cheersh,' I say in my best Sean Connery, 'tonight we shail into hishtory.'

'Channeling Sean Connery are we? says Deborah Slur. Deborah, you may, or not be aware, is the arts correspondent for the London based SoWhat! Magazine.

SoWhat! pride themselves on their extensive arts listings and coverage, and D.attends all the openings, usually ending up being fucked in a toilet. D., knew nothing about art which didn't stop her from having an opinion.

'Dave!' Shouted D. from less than two feet away. Everyone stopped and looked over at us, even D.A on decks paused the music.

D.A. was previewing his new musical Dwarfz which was essentially bite sized chunks of music recorded at low levels from samples taken of conversations between dwarfs and regular people, mixed and looped with background noise. J.H. had created a cartoon strip for the album from which D.A. was choreographing his stage version which was scheduled to open the Royal Opera House's new Autumn programme.

'What do you want Deborah?' I said this with barely concealed contempt which the bitch took as an invite to join me

'Isn't it wonderful?'

'No it isn't. It's fucking Disneyland without the gravitas, you ignorant halfwit.'

'Oh! I don't know Dave.'

'I know you don't. You've got to ask yourself one question: where's the fucking art?' D. looked perplexed, I wrestled two Becks and a bottle of vodka from a dwarf on a skateboard. 'Next time,' I quietly informed him, 'bring me a bottle of chloroform and a cosh, I have an arts writer to kill.'

J. And D. shuffle over having deposited K.M. with N.C. 'that should set the cat among the dandelions,' said J. 'Hello Deborah,' they said with a smile that suggested perversions, in the name of art, were imminent and that she was the canvas.

'Boys!' She smiled back. D. didn't know what she was getting herself into. 'What atrocities are you working on. I hear Clive Barker wants to buy the new work, sight unseen. Want to give me an exclusive?' 'Too late, I thought.'

'We'd love to,' said J. and D., taking D.S. by each elbow and leading her toward the toilets.

'Dave, don't forget, River Café 1pm. Friday. Ciao.'

I had, come to think of it, but the thought of lunch on SoWhat! Magazine, made an hour with D. bearable. Or did it? She wanted an interview to publicise my forthcoming exhibition and a photo for the cover with, according to her email, a piece from the show exclusively in the background. Not a fucking chance, I think. But, if I arrive an hour or so early, I could eat and be on my way out by the time she arrived.

I was smiling, probably inanely and drooling slightly when Lord GaGa began shaking me by the hand splashing vodka everywhere. 'Goddamn brilliant! Brilliant. I think I'll buy the whole goddamn show!'

'What fucking show? This is not a fucking show!' By now I was screaming. 'Where's the art? Show me the fucking art!'

There was a small crowd gathered around me which spontaneously broke into applause. They actually believed I was part of the event. Motherfuckers! I thought, reaching for my mock Glock. As I was about to unleash the full force of Dirty Harry at them. 'Well do you Punk?' The gallery doors swing open and G. and G. enter wearing matching Autumn coloured suits and yellow silk ties and in perfect formation march around the inner perimeter of the gallery and out the way they came in, and without breaking stride enter a black cab which immediately drives off.

And I swear G. looked through the cab window and mouthed, 'Candy's waiting.' Or it could have been 'Camden. My good man.'

Anyway, I didn't need this...this wankfest. I needed to sleep, and grabbing a couple of beers from a passing dwarf, I left through a bathroom window.

Excerpts from an Artist's (so-called) life...

Trespassers will not be prosecuted

Questions were torturing me as I walked up Wardour Street. My gaff? Anybody else's gaff? A bench in Russell Square Gardens? What did it all mean. And then bingo! Answers-still haven't found my front door keys. If I knock someone up they'll want to talk and the conversation will inevitably lead to my exhibition-fuckers! So the answer to the question where am I going to sleep was a bench in the gardens. By the time I'd worked this out, I was walking along Great Russell Street, and with two bounds, lanky fucker that I am, I was over the railings. Laying on a bench under a horse chestnut tree and covering myself with the Gallery X catalogue, which I'd lifted from a dwarf's back pocket as I left, curiosity got the better of me. Opening the cover, on which it simply said Catalogue Gallery X, I thumbed through 30 white pages, all of them blank. There was nothing in it. There was fuck all in it. No fuckingthing. Typical.

Downing the two bottles of Becks, I fell asleep to the sound of traffic on the Euston Road. 'Excuse me Sir.' I opened one eye and spied two Old Bill standing over me. Looking at my watch. 10 past 8. Breakfast I thought. 'Excuse me Sir.'

My god these plods are were persistent. 'Are you talking to me?'

'Yes we are Sir. Are you aware these are private gardens and sleeping here is not allowed.'

'What the fuck are you talking about? Can't you hear my breakfast calling to me?' The plods look at each other. I push them apart and stride out to familiar parts. The Old Bill meanwhile were left trying to out stare each other. Neither willing to blink. They'd be there all morning until a goddamn tourist asks them for directions.

Excerpts from an Artist's (so-called) life...

I'm ready for my close-up

Sitting at a table outside Maison Berteaux breakfasting on four espressos and six brioche. I consider for a moment going to my studio in Fitzrovia. The work can't wait. My muse is restrained, while I, a plaything of agents, galleryists, pundits interviewers, critics and other assorted cunts, have to play along. Or do I? Do I fuck! I'll play it my way. I feel her strain against her bonds. I have canvases to assault! But first an interview with A.G.D., for the so-called Culture Show.

I order more espresso and even more brioche. As I'm lighting a schmoke, Noel Fielding pulls up on a cherry red BMX, chains it to my table, helps himself to a brioche which he dunks into my coffee and bounds into the café spitting crumbs and shouting, 'cheers,' over his shoulder. Funny geezer, I think, he can come over and doodle me anytime. Come over and doodle anytime, I mean. Shaking free of my reverie, I look up to see A.G.D. climb out of a cab and boyishly throw his hair back. 'Dave hi,' he says offering me his hand. This is Sheila my stylist, I mean researcher. She's prepared a number of questions, which I'll leave with you to read through. Because, Dave, you're worth it.'

A camera crew and sound engineer set up their equipment around me. While a street lunatic mirrors their movements. Or he could be a fucking mime. I think is there a difference? Then it occurs to me that street lunatics have their reasons.

This one was now informing the camera man that zombies live in the Underground and he should know as he is a zombie himself. Admittedly he did look a little ashen faced. One of the crew offered him a £5 note to get himself a cup of tea, just as A.G.D. and Noel Fielding walk out out of the café. 'Wash rinse and wash again,' said A.G.D. 'for that flyaway look.'

'Fanx man,' says Noel unchaining his BMX. Pausing only to flick his hair over his shoulder, he pedals towards Shaftesbury Avenue, followed by the street lunatic running on all fours and barking.

A.G.D. standing on the pavement waves after him shouting, 'because you're worth it.' Taking a seat opposite me A.G.D. takes a sip of Evian, nods to the camera guy to roll and says, 'so Dave, what product do you use on your hair?'

Three of the crew have to pull me off a now bleeding A.G.D. Shaking free I continue pounding the fucker with a Martini ashtray. If it's not Brian Sewell, who makes Prince Charles sound common, with his rants against contemporary art and artists, it's A.G.D. who can't walk past a shiny surface without checking his profile.

Excerpts from an Artist's (so-called) life...

Is that your final answer?

   Noon o'clock interview with R.R. from ArtoGo Magazine. I'm schmoking a Gitane and drinking my seventh espresso in Paul's on Old Compton Street. A group of tourists are complaining to the waiter about me. 'It's against the law!' 'Shouldn't be allowed!' 'How do you get to Leicester Square?' 'Where's my wallet?' Pete shows them the door.
   'Good riddance,' I say as he walks over, 'fucking tourists!'
   'You've made your point Dave. You can stop smoking now, they've fucked off.'
   R.R. meanwhile has sat down at the table opposite me. He lays out a notepad, tape recorder, and four classic green Pentel rollerballs. He then takes eight miniature bottles of vodka out of his satchel pours them into two glasses, hands me one and downs his in one gulp.
   'So Dave,' he says, 'you're often called the 'Poet of Insanity,' and were recently quoted as saying that you have a murder/suicide pact with your work. How do you address these, some would say, accusations?'
   Feeling a nerve twitch in my left eye, I call his bluff. Answers. Fuck answers. I dive into my bag and pull out a bottle of Stoli. 'Call it!' I say. I notice his his left eye beginning to blink. He slams his empty glass down saying, 'Hit me.' I fill both our glasses and together we knock back the contents. I refill the glasses.

'Mr Rabid. Rufus,' I say. 'The truth would make your eyes bleed. And, before you ask, there is no truth to the rumour that I plagiarized K.M's work and tortured his dog.' Although considering the barking and yelping that permeates my nightmares, I'm not so sure.

'But,' says R.R. I wave my hand for him to continue. 'You said the last time we spoke that, 'Creating art is about ability and criminal enterprise.' What exactly do you mean?'

Topping up our glasses,, I fix him with a stare. Both of us not blinking. There is a clock ticking somewhere in the café and Ennio Morricone playing on someone's car stereo outside. The café goes quiet, our eyes start to twitch in unison. I break the spell. 'I was being artistically ironic. Rufus.' R.R. starts to breath again, swallows his vodka and dives into his bag emerging with a bottle of Absolut. Topping up our glasses to polite applause from people seated around us and the usual assortment of tourists, morists and borists, R.R. opens his mouth to say something. But before he can utter a word I say, 'Or was I?'

The café crowd goes wild. There is much whooping from the regular patrons. Pete comes over with a tray of warm brioche. R.R. taking a brioche in one hand and a pen in the other starts making copious notes, washing down the brioche with the remains of the vodka.

'Long live propaganda,' I say getting up and nodding to Pete. The sun blazing down on Old Compton Street revives me and I think, 'time for a drink!'

Excerpts from an Artist's (so-called) life...

Living in the fast lane

'Ten pints and then home for a piss,' I tell the geezer behind the bar. The sixth London Pride goes down as good as the first. 'Forget going home for a piss,' I say, ordering another pair of pints. 'I'll be back in three minutes,' and lurch towards the toilets.

Lost in the act of making swirling patterns with the piss stream, I fail to notice a tall leggy blonde. That is, until she whispers in my ear, 'Do you realise this is the ladies and you're watering the the plants?'

'For fuck's sake!' I exclaim, thinking she's wearing Diorissimo. Zipping myself up I say, 'Join me for a drink?' And 'I'm Dave.' And. 'Lurch this way.' I know I'm fucking rambling but she's intoxicating an already intoxicated me.

At the bar she orders a vodka and tonic and another pair of pints for me. And I order a bag of peanuts, a bag of tomato sauce flavour crisps, a packet of pork scratchings, a tube of sour cream flavour Pringles and another pair of pints.

The bar guy piles the snax in front of me. I down a London Pride and start to nosh down. I feel a tap on my shoulder, looking up I eyeball the blonde looking down at me. 'Oh! Fuck,' I think. I'd forgotten about her. 'Hi,' I say straitening up and brushing crisps from my shirt, 'I'm Dave.'

'I think we've ascertained that. Do you want to be reminded who I am?'

I momentarily think about tossing a coin. Heads, ask her name. Tails, eat the nuts. She takes the decision out of my hands. 'It's Celine. And you don't remember me do you?'

Playing for time, I down another pint. And suddenly it comes back to me. 'I remember,' I say, 'I met you in the toilet.'

She looks at me like I'm Nick Clegg. 'Before today, you muppet!'

'Er...No,' I say, picking up the Pringles, 'want one?'

'No thanks. We met last month at T.E's preview at the White Cube. You were wearing linen, I was wearing leather. I suggested you paint me in the nude. You said you always sleep with your models. I said okay, let's go back to your place. Your reply was to hand me your empty glass of vodka, saying you'd be back in a moment. That was four weeks ago. What the fuck happened?'

As I pondered this, Celine ordered two more pints and a double vodka and tonic and sat on the bar stool. I couldn't help noticing she was wearing a white thong. She noticed me looking and opened her legs wider.

'Well? What happened?'

'It's all a blur,' I say. 'The last thing I remember is T. asking me how the work for my show was coming along and then nothing until I woke up in a garden in Holland Park surrounded by dwarfs.'

She stood up, 'Christ she's tall,' I thought, that is until she bent down and pulled me off the floor. I must have slid down the bar, but, fuck me, she was still at least six inches taller than me, and I'm 5'10."

'You're tall,' I say, 'wanna come back to my studio and I'll paint you wearing a gas mask?'

'You're talking my language,' she says, spritzing herself with Diorissimo. 'I'll take a moment to freshen up, you hail us a taxi.'

Time for another pint while she's in the loo, I think. Carrying a London Pride with me I stand on the kerb looking for a yellow light. A mini-cab spots me, does a U-turn and pulls up alongside ignoring angry blasts of horn from other cars he's cut up. He winds his window down pops his head out saying 'I speak no English, you speak no English, I drive you longtime big boy. Where to?'

'The Box.' I say, feeling anxious, sure I've forgotten something. Noticing the London Pride in my hand, I breathe out, beginning to relax. 'Come to daddy,' I say, 'I haven't forgotten you,' taking a five finger slurp.

The mini-cab driver of no-fixed nationality is looking in the side mirror saying to himself. 'Who's the daddy? Who's the daddy?' Waving his hands and driving with his knees. By the time the police pull us over we're on Archer Street. I think 30 seconds walk to The Box or wait for another cab? The mini-cab driver now being manhandled into the back of the police car is screaming, 'I'm the daddy, I'm the daddy!'

Finishing the pint, I hand the empty glass to one of the Old Bill saying, 'Bag it and tag it! It's evidence!' And walk across the road to the roped-off entrance.

Excerpts from an Artist's (so-called) life...

Heeeeeeeeere's Johnny

   The old Raymond Revue building never looked so good or so exclusive. A face-management team on the door were working from a Blackberry of names and corresponding photo I.D.ing who could or couldn't go in. 'Hi,' I said, 'I'm a friend of Mr Hammerstein.'
   'Fuck off!'
   'I'm Dave Rogers a friend of the family.'
   'Fuck off!'
   And then. Suddenly. 'He's with me.'
   Fuck me! It's Deborah Slur. Losing the will to argue, I allow her to take me by the hand and lead me in. She checks in her Westwood cape, I check in my balaclava. The coat-check girl gives me a number and as I take it, I notice her name badge. 'Brandy.' A feeling of déjà-vu washes over me and then I'm standing under a giant pineapple.
   'It's so now!' Debs intones taking a photograph of it with her phone. Taking two glasses of Cristel from an obliging waitress, I drink them both and follow her to the bar. A Debbie Harry clone behind the bar puts two glasses and a bottle of champagne down and the waitress, who I notice also looks like Debbie Harry, fills them up, offers me one and takes one herself.
   'This is New York in London,' she says, 'it's the new Studio 54.'

From a doorway a white horse, with a semi-naked V.B. riding on it clip-clops onto the dance floor. Studio 54 my arse, I think, noticing a sign to the bathroom. Picking up the champagne bottle by the neck, and briefly flashing to an image of D.S. throat, I walk towards the toilets. D.S. calls out, 'Don't forget the interview,' as I push the door open. After taking a long and languorous piss, I climb out of the toilet window, thinking 'been there, done that,' and successfully failed to buy the tee shirt. Don't these fuckers know it's been done before. Warhol would be turning in his wig.

Hitting the street, I walk to my gaff. Turning a corner I spot Martin a local street lunatic. 'How's it going M?' I say, handing him the bottle of warm champagne.

'Good. Thanks. How's the exhibition coming along?' M. was a burn out from the 80s, an original master of the universe. Trading stocks and shares and snorting coke 24/7. He experienced a drug induced encounter after hoovering too many lines, with a personage who looked a lot like old man Steptoe, who informed him he was just a rag and bone man getting above himself. Waking up, looking like an iced cake in red braces, he realised Steptoe was right in his assessment and walked out, never to set foot in the Square Mile again. Instead making a successful alternate career of sleeping on front door steps, protecting them from being pissed on by other street lunatics. The only drawback was a 4am tourettes shout of 'Harold!' and the smell of piss emanating off him. 'It's coming along. Protect my door M.' I say letting myself in and flopping onto the bed.

All night I'm plagued by dreams of synchronized barn dancing. Staged by dwarfs and Lowry's stick men to a soundtrack of *'Lucy in the Sky with Diamonds.'* A melange of styles, if you will? Will you?

Picture yourself in a barge on the Manchester Ship Canal
With mill chimneys spewing into slate grey skies
Somebody whistles you, you answer quite slowly
'hey chuck!'
A tall geezer with clouds round his eyes
Take your partner by the hand,
tap his head and spin him around.

Hour after hour of spinning dwarfs and lofty fuckers in a landscape all shades of gray. I wake late with a raging thirst and a hard-on. Celine, I think. Blank canvas, I think. Another day of interviews, I think. What the fuck, I think.

Excerpts from an Artist's (so-called) life...

Not tested on animals

A plan began to coalesce in my mind. Avoid the studio. The canvas can wait a little longer, there are still so many weeks? Days? left until the opening night.

NOTE TO SELF: Speak to Gallery. When do I open?

Stepping over M. I slip a folded £5 note into a piss soaked pocket. His snoring is punctuated with a 'Thanks man.'

Waving down a cab, 'River Café.' I say and spend the next 20 minutes organising my day. Early lunch at the River Café. Followed by lunch at the River Café. Fuck it! Why not give D.S. an interview, I think, I'll be fortified by my pre-lunch lunch. And I'll be ready for lunch and two hours of talking bollocks. All this thinking about lunch has made me hungry. Just in time we pull up outside the café entrance, as I was contemplating jumping out at the next set of lights and hoofing it in search of a street burger.

'I'm..? I'm..?' I say to the maitre de, having momentarily forgotten who I am. He narrows his eyes and suspicion clouds his face. 'Ah!' I say, I'm a guest of SoWhat! Magazine. He shrugs his shoulders, beckons 'follow me,' and leads me to a table. Handing me a menu he asks, 'would sir like an aperitif?'

'A bottle of Newcastle Brown,' I say, and hold the glass.' Necking the Newcastle B. expertly delivered to my table, I peruse the menu. 'God,' I think this takes me back to the days I was working here in the kitchen with J.O. Now, when I say working in the kitchen, I mean washing-up in the kitchen. It was a summer job before my star rose, just before, in fact, I sold my first painting to C.S. Chuck went on to buy my next 16 paintings on the first night of my first exhibition held in an empty shop on the Walworth Road. A first for me and speaking of thirst, I order another bottle of Newcastle B.

'Many's the afternoon,' I say to the waitress, who's taking the top off the bottle of NewB. with a bottle opener and offering it to me to sniff, nice touch I think. 'Anyway,' I continue, 'J.O. and yours truly would skive around the back with a crate of these brown beauties and plan our respective futures. What ever you do J., I said, don't sell out. Don't take the corporate shilling to get your face on television or be the face of Spar. Be true to your mockney Italian roots. And do you know what he said? Of course you don't, I was just being polite. He said fuck all, he was too busy being sick all over his Converse sneakers. But look at him now. Still can't drink.'

The waitress, I note, was toying with the bottle cap, considering self-harm or taking my order. I think she'd listened to too many stories.

'Would you like to order now?' She asks, 'before I throw myself on the wood-burning oven.'

'Yep.' I say, 'I'll have the entire antipasti menu and three bottles of Soave Classico 'La Rocca' 2008.' Slurping and chomping, 45 minutes pass like ¾ of an hour and then I'm interrupted by a shrill 'Dave!' 'Fuck me', I think.'

'Fuck me,' says the waitress, 'I knew I recognised you. You're the artist that always paints...' Pushing the waitress out of the way D.S. takes a seat opposite me pours herself a glass of wine from one of the opened bottles and says, 'two more bottles of whatever he's drinking and the menu, if you would be so kind.' The waitress considers this request for a moment, and acts on it, walking purposefully to the kitchen. D.S. meanwhile, has taken out a notepad, from her Mulberry handbag, and what appears to be a piece of chalk which she's finding it difficult to write with. 'Piece of shit,' she whines, shaking it vigorously.

'Debs,' I say, 'that's a tampon and unless you intend writing in red, I'd suggest you use a pen instead.'

Looking at her hand holding the tampon; looking at me; looking back at the tampon and finally looking at the waitress, who by now has returned with our wine and menus, she shakes her head and parks the tampon behind her right ear, like a cigarette. 'Dave,' she purrs, 'order for both of us will you. I'm going to the little girls room.' And fishing a lighter from her bag she exits stage right.

The waitress pen poised takes the hint and says, 'what'll it be?'

'Well,' I say, not needing to read the menu as I'd decided earlier, 'we'll both have antipasti of Puntarelle alla Romana* (*thinly sliced cicoria shoots with anchovy chili and red wine vinegar) followed by primi of Risotto con Aragosta* (*with lobster, parsley and Prosecco) and secondi of Capesante in pudella* (*Scottish scallops seared with fresh chili, capers, sage and lemon with kyle, mache and Castelluccio lentils) and four bottles of the 'La Rocca' 2008 please.

She smiles, taps her pen on the pad and says, 'if I'm not being to forward...'

'Too late,' I say.

'...do you want to paint me in the nude?' She hands me a slip of paper with a phone number written on it, a smiley face, the name Sara and an X.

Folding it in half, I slide it into my bag whilst giving her the fingers in the ear and mouth 'call you' sign. As she crosses the restaurant she passes the manager coming the other way holding D. by the arm. Stopping at the table he says, looking at me with a stare of a man who'd thought he'd seen it all, 'this person claims she is with you. Can you confirm or deny this before we call the police.'

'Deborah is nodding at me like she's practicing for a blow-job. 'Why do you ask?' I say.

'We had complaints from customers that there was a deranged woman trying to smoke a tampon in the bathroom.'

'Call the police!' I say. 'Call the police now!'

Two hours later, after having eaten both our meals and finished the wine and ordering an espresso to go, I ask a waiter to book me a taxi on account. He asks me, not unreasonably, who is paying for lunch?

'SoWhat! Magazine,' I inform him, whose representative you have had arrested.'

He looks at me aghast, and actually says, would you fucking believe it, 'Moi?'

'Yes. You.' I say taking my espresso from the proffered hand of a waitress. Walking past the manager to my waiting taxi, I stop and shake his hand, 'Good work today, good work. If she shows up again shoot her. It will be a mercy killing. And don't let the magazine stiff you for the bill.' With that I climb into the taxi, calling back, 'don't forget to add a tip to it for yourself,' I conclude as the driver asks, 'where to?'

'I'm glad you asked me that question.' I say.

Excerpts from an Artist's (so-called) life...

A means to an end

'Get it over with,' I think, arriving outside the offices of ArtPimp© who have organised, with the help of my dealer, a panel of critics and other mouthfrothers in a question and answer session about my new work and forthcoming show. A crew from BBC radio are also on hand to record it for later broadcast.

A concierge opens the door, 'Hi Dave,' he says.

'My dog!' I say. 'Alan how are you?'

'Good, man, but not as good as you apparently. Be careful it's a mosh pit of critics up there and they're looking for blood. Your blood.'

'Fanx. What floor?'

'6th.'

'See you on the way out? Drink?'

'Yep,' he says and hands me the remains of a spliff. The remains being two inches long. Taking the stairs and stopping at each flight for a drag, I arrive in reception 40 minutes later.

Clive, my dealer and owner of the gallery where my work is shown, meets me at the top of the stairs. 'Where the fuck have you...' He stops himself, takes a breath and says, 'Good to see you Dave. Need anything before we start? Everything is set up and we're using some of your previous work as backdrops.'

My breathing settles down to a pant and I say, 'Coffee Clive. Get me a goddamn coffee.' He leads me into a room typically ArtPimp©, 60s retro furniture, bold red and white patterns on the walls mixed with flat screen televisions on every wall, three Gaggia coffee machines steaming. And in the middle of all this was a B.B.C. Crew; M.H. Arts critic for the Kulture section of a Sunday broadsheet; Akira Lau owner of ArtPimp©, who apparently was chairing this Q+A session; Susie Smith from Fork IT©, a new arts magazine specialising in in erotik art; Clive: and finally the Dunn brothers, pundits who claim to know what's coming up in the art world by keeping their ears to the ground. And presumably listening to a lot of dog shit.

Excerpts from an Artist's (so-called) life...

For the benefit of the recording

Akira taps his coffee cup for attention, gets it and sits back down on his Joe Colombo chair. 'Before we begin,' he says, 'my secretary Marsha has strict instructions to call the police at the first signs of violence or weapons discharge. Dave, this means you as well. OK?'

Not actually having listened I nod an OK. Taking three cups I pour double espressos in each and sit down.

M.H. looks at me, 'You were recently quoted as saying that when you meet your critics you go in weapons hot. What do you actually mean by this and how does implied violence ingratiate yourself and your work with the wider public?'

'When you say wider public Mickey, are you, in fact, implying that the occasional fat bastard who sees my work will feel threatened?'

Akira looks over at the BBC producer, who says, 'we can take it out in the editing.'

'Can I,' says M.H. 'point out my name is Michael. I will not tolerate the shortening of it. It implies lack of due deference and respect for me and my position.'

'Fuck me! That's fucking told me Mick. Although I think one of us has maybe lost the plot. And I think it's you Micky baby.'

Akira raises his arms and then lowers them gently.

Everyone takes a breath. The producer gives him the OK sign. Looking at M.H. Akira bows slightly and says, 'I take responsibility for this dishonour and will ensure it does not reoccur Mickey San. No! I mean Mike, no Mick, no Micky. Oh Fuck!'

Maybe, I think, it's Akira who's lost the plot.

M.H. Now purple in the face, gets up and walks out.

I drink the coffee and make three more cups, while one of the BBC. team tries and fails to encourage M.H. back into the recording session. 'I'm sorry,' she says on her return, 'M.H. will not be participating any longer. He also informed me that we cannot use any of the material recorded prior to him leaving and that we would be hearing from his lawyers if we do. 'In that case I'll see you in court' I said, to which he replied, 'fucking modern art, Brian was correct all along,' and he then stormed out kicking over potted palm trees on his way to the elevator.

Akira, having regained control, says 'Dave, your last exhibition was a sell-out, the public loved it, M.F. from Sky Arts gushed, the Observer did a feature on you. But the critics, M.H. for one, ignored your work. Does this upset or even annoy you?'

Drinking all three cups of coffee in the requisite two slurps per cup and taking from my inside pocket two miniature bottles of vodka, I pour them into one of the empty cups. Looking at Akira, I say, 'as the question doesn't interest me, I'll let Clive field this one.' I then remember sitting back and sipping the vodka. And...

Apparently, Susie informed me, having prodded me in the ribs to wake me up, I'd gone into a deep sleep and spent 20 minutes snoring loudly while Clive justified his 40%.

The Dunn brothers, in a pincer movement, ask, 'Dave, all of your work is of women, and many critics, especially us, believe it is exploitative. Do you believe your work has any artistic merit?'

Just as I'm reaching for my mock Glock, Susie says, 'speaking as a critic and a women Dave, you can exploit me anytime.'

She then takes my hand and leads me out. 'Not the elevator!' I say. 'Not the goddamn elevator!'

Excerpts from an Artist's (so-called) life...

Lead us into temptation

   Reaching the ground floor. S.S. asks, 'your studio or my apartment? Paint me or tie me to the four corners of the bed and lay me! Make your mind up by the time I've got the car.'
   She then bends over for absolutely no reason at all, and lingers for a moment. Alan, walking out of one of the offices, takes one look at her bum in a mini-skirt and, walking into a desk, trips and bangs his head on the floor. Now I understand. I shout after her as she's pushing through the revolving doors, 'Have you any bondage rope?'
   'Yes.' She calls back.
   'Your place then.' I shout. 'And hurry.'
   Alan walks over rubbing his head. 'Alan,' I say, 'about that drink...'
   'No probs. I completely understand. Rain check?' He pushes open the door onto Marylebone High Street as S.S. pulls up outside. 'By the way,' he says, 'I'm showing my found sculptures on Sunday, 12 hours only, come rain or shine on Clapham Common, see if you can make it.'
   'I'll do my best,' I say climbing into S's Smart car.

Excerpts from an Artist's (so-called) life...

Not suitable for children

[**Editor's Note:** Due to the unrestrained and graphic detail
of this excerpt, it has been decided to only print a
list of points covered in the text.]

Bondage rope. Gag. Latex. Riding crop. Vodka. Nipple clamps.
Marshmallows. Peanut M+Ms.

Excerpts from an Artist's (so-called) life...

Burger King revolutionary

Waking-up 24 hours later in S's bed in Balham, I consider for a moment going back to sleep. That is until S. straight from the shower, jumps on the bed. Smiling like a loon and falling into my arms she says, "Dave! Gotta go. We drank all the alcohol and there's no food left. Don't forget to close the door behind you when you leave. AND don't forget you said you'd paint me nude for the exhibition. AND if you want to do this again, bring some leg spreaders with you next time.

Bouncing off the bed and pouring herself into a latex dress, she's dressed in under two minutes. 'It's been real,' she says, winking and closing the door behind her.

I'm thinking, 'FOOD GODDAMN IT!' And I want it fast. Fast food. Jumping into my clothes and climbing out of the bathroom window, I make my way to the nearest Burger King.

'Six Royales with cheese. Eight portions of fries. Two vanilla milkshakes. And four coffees. Please.' I say to the three gold starred kid behind the counter.

Taking my money and staring at me, just a little too long, he makes a connexion in his head and says, 'Now I remember! You're that artist that was photographed sitting in a deckchair on a roundabout, in Kilburn at rush hour, with a nude woman at your feet.'

'Yep!' I say, 'that was me. How did you get to see that?'
'Well...'
'Talk fast kid, I'm off to the outdoor sculpture event on Clapham Common in an hour.'
'My sister showed it to me, she always buys The Observer.'
'What did she say kid?'
'That she wanted to be the woman at your feet.'
'Kid.' I say. 'how old is she?'
'23.'
Taking a card from my pocket, I say, 'give this to your sister, and ask her to call me.'
Picking-up two trays with my food piled up and only stopping to fill the coffee cups. I sit down at a table and chomp down on the burger bad boys. Catching the kid's eye and calling him over I say, 'Kid! I'll have the same again.'

Excerpts from an Artist's (so-called) life...

Do walk on the grass

   Still feeling peckish I make my way to Clapham Common via a kebab shop on the High Street. 20 minutes and two doners later, feeling replete but still missing something. 'I think a pint! Or perhaps two of London Pride would go down a treat.' After picking up and wiping my mouth with a Chihuahua being walked by an Au-pair, I enter an insalubrious bar and order two pints of Pride. 'Good.' I think, 'but not good enough.' Perhaps another pair of pints followed by a leisurely stroll to the open air event.
   Described by SoWhat! Magazine as an;

**'Arts Festival to rival anything
Tate Modern or the South Bank can produce.
Bringing together music, literature, art,
poetry and sculpture.
With workshops, organic food outlets and a
creative crèche experience for children to explore their
inner artist.
"A 12 hour event: A lifetime of memories."
© 2011 SoWhat! Magazine.**

What SoWhat! failed to mention was that they were funding the whole event as a loss leader to add credibility to their magazine and boost an ailing circulation.

My concern was who they would send to cover it. Walking onto the Common, past stall after stall of artisan food; tofu pies, organic burgers, ice-creams, freshly milked cow juice, I stop at La Buggermoi, take a sample of bread and dip it into the complimentary oil. 'Interesting taste,' I say to the assistant, 'what is it?'

'A combination of flour, water and yeast, simples innit!'

'You mean bread. And the oil?'

'Castroli Getex.'

'Interesting. I'll try the wine and cheese.' Being a connoisseur of wine from years of attending exhibition openings, which in my younger days I'd crash just for the free food; wine, cheese and crisps, sod the art, I needed the sustenance to do my own work.

Sipping the wine, swilling it around my teeth, gargling and spitting into the oil dish, I top up the glass and bite into a slab of cheese. Chewing, gnashing and finally gobbing the semi-masticated goo into the oil dish I say, 'Fuck me squire. That was an experience.'

The assistant looks at me and says, 'so me old china, what do you think?'

The fucker asked me, so what could I do, 'I'll see what I can do,' I say. 'The wine has a flavour profile that hints of Bazooka Joe and notes of melon, old copies of the Sun and reeks of week old P.G.Tips teabags. On the palate it's hairy to the point of being compared to an old sock, but then opens out into, what can only be described as council estate East Croydon circa 1976. Its effervescent head keeping the flavours just the wrong side of authentic. In the mouth it tastes like roadkill after heavy rain, sun, and heavy rain again.'

By now a reporter from the Metro has wandered over to see what the fuss is all about. 'Hi,' she says, 'you're that artist, Dave...' Before she can say anymore, she is interrupted by an incensed stall holder.

'He knows fuck all about wine, ask him what he knows about cheese.' and follows this through with a chant of 'Tosser! Tosser! Tosser!'

'Well,' says the reporter, 'let's record this for my piece on the festival for next Thursday's edition,'

Turning and pointing to the cheese I say, 'here we have a local variety of hard cheese originating from a shed in the back garden of a house off the Mile End Road. It has probably been made by the same family for the last 12 hours. Long on the tongue, sharp, like a barbed comment made by your girlfriends mother on meeting you for the first time. Oily and intense without any subtlety at all, this cheese fell off the back of a lorry on its way here. Claiming to be something it's not. This cheese crosses social barriers like a burp and will compliment a can of Special Brew.

Pouring the glass of wine back into the bottle and stuffing a napkin into the neck. I step several paces back, and taking out my Zippo, light the napkin and throw the bottle into the stall, which ignites into a fireball. The assistant, meanwhile, has legged it.

'Well that's a dramatic ending to my piece,' says the Metro reporter. 'Where are you off to now?'

'The Sculpture Garden,' I say.

'Mind if I tag along?'

'Nope! I'll introduce you to the sculptor.'

Excerpts from an Artist's (so-called) life...

Reporting live from...

Passing large blocks of stone, wood and even polystyrene all of them with strategically placed holes and indentations, paying homage to Henry Moore, we enter a space filled with Alan's street sculpture.

'My god!' Says the reporter, 'what is this?'

Alan strolling over says, 'It's found sculpture. This piece I call Skip. Which, in fact, it is. A skip!'

The reporter looks at it, looks at Alan and says, 'It's a skip full of building materials...'

'Exactly. I stole it from outside a house in Dulwich.'

'And this?'

'A shopping trolley I fished out of the canal in Camden, tentatively titled Dumped Trolley.'

'And this?'

'A McDonald's street bin from outside their restaurant in Woolwich. This one I call Street Sign.'

The reporter looks at it nailed to a tree and says to Alan. 'Abbey Road!'

Alan by now is beaming and lights up a Wandsworth Wonder, a spliff the size of the common. A roach by any other name. Taking a drag, so deep and so long, that it appears to slow down time itself, he slowly exhales and whispers, 'Dave?'

'Thanx man,' I say, remembering I'm a joker, a smoker, a midnight toker. I drag so deep that my cheekbones look even more chiseled. I hand the roach to the reporter, who to Alan's amazement, finishes it off in two lungfuls, flipping the remains into the skip.

Alan, clearly impressed, waves his hands in front of her face, which has the desired effect. The reporter refocusing, breathes saying, 'and these?'

'These are from my new series I call Signs. This is my latest triptych Powis Street, Brompton Road and the pièce de résistance No Parking. It says it all really.'

'What does it say?'

'It all.'

The reporter still feeling the effects of the 2Ws writes it all down.

'And finally,' says Alan, my latest piece, I call Indesit Washing Machine Kaput!'

'Er?'

'This I came across while I was walking through Crystal Palace Park at four in the morning. I'd just shared a 2Ws with a family of gnomes that live by the lake, nice enough but they follow you home and ring the doorbell all night. You open the window to shoo them away and they hide and, would you believe it, five minutes later Ding Dong! Ding Ding! Anyway, I notice the moon glinting off something in the bushes and there it is, a homage to built-in obsolescence.'

The reporter turns off her tape recorder, mutters something about bloody gnomes, turns to Alan and says, 'I have the munchies. I require chocolate and Guinness. Come and partake with me or naff off!' She then slides down the Indesit and sits on the grass giggling.

Alan shrugs his shoulders, says, 'why not? You coming Dave?'

I consider my options; an evening of quaffing and laughing in convivial company or more importantly getting back to my studio and working on my pieces for the exhibition. 'No contest,' I think. 'Alan.' I say, 'and whatever your name is. Ms Metro. Let us repair to the Madame JoJo's for an evening of cabaret and black velvet.

Excerpts from an Artist's (so-called) life...

Come on baby light my fire

Deviant Vivika was teasing the audience with a mix of burlesque and striptease. M.L.Y. was in the audience shouting, 'Get yer tits out for the lads.' And was providing as much entertainment as D.V. until he was forcedly ejected. His loud claims of, 'This is a performance, I'm a poet, don't you know it!' Were largely ignored. We, on the other hand, applauded loudly calling for an éncore and more black velvet.

Out of nowhere Ms Metro says to Alan, 'I've been thinking, and this is my last question before one of you takes me home. Having set up your sculpture garden what happens to the exhibits when the show is over?'

Alan drains his black velvet asks for three pints of Guinness. Wiping his mouth on the tablecloth, as he eschews napkins as petite-bourgeoisie, says, 'my work is about forceable relocation. I repatriate sculpture from one location to another location, where it remains until someone else moves it again.'

Ms Metro, clicking her pen off and placing it and the notebook in her bag, takes a sip from the Guinness. D.V. is on stage, coming to the end of her show, fan dancing and looking over at our table. She points at me and winks as a waiter appears with an envelope. Handing him a perfectly folded £5 note, I take the envelope. Inside is a sky blue piece of paper and written on it in ultramarine ink it says:

You're the artist who was
born to paint me.
Your brush. My body.
Meet me at the bar
at midnight. D.V.

'That's decided who's taking Ms Metro home,' I think. Alan is intrigued. Spontaneous applause erupts all around us. I consider for a moment standing up and taking a bow, but modesty prevails.

'What did it say?' queries Alan.

'D.V. asking if I'll hang around and have a drink with her.'

'She could be your next subject.'

'I know. I'm thinking of painting her draped across the bonnet of a black Ford Capri, circa 1973, faux sexy calendar shot.'

Alan grins and turning to Ms Metro says, 'your place via the hot dog stand on Piccadilly Circus. You keep him talking, I'll leg it with the stand.'

Ms Metro, seeing a climatic ending to her article, nods and slaps on some Mac Russian Red lippy. 'Let's keep in touch,' she says, 'rumour has it that you're opening a new show. I could cover it for the Arts page of Metro, and don't forget, I'm always available for you if you want to paint me naked.'

'Fanx.' I say as she and Alan get up.

'Later,' says Alan.

'Innit!' I say, bumping knuckles with him.

As I'm watching them leave a geezer comes over to me and introducing himself as Brad, says, 'Hi fella, I'm one of Ms Vivika's management team. One of my many responsibilities is Public Relations and the strategic placing of positive material about her in the press.

I believe that you live an eccentric, somewhat bohemian lifestyle, which may impact Ms. Vivika's credibility. And it is on that basis that I ask you not to meet with her this evening.'

Looking at Brad, I say, 'there's three things you need to know about me. One; I don't like elevators, two; I hate PR. And three; I hate PR.'

Brad, looking a little confused, takes out a Blackberry and starts to type. 'I believe,' he says earnestly, 'that point two and three are the same. Point three in fact is otiose.'

'Friedrich Nietzsche said that 'Art is the proper task of life.' Which Brad, is why I am compelled to follow my muse wherever she leads me, and often she leads me into temptation.

Brad's face betrays a brief eclipse of fear, which he quickly alters to a serious, 'I'm in control visage.' 'What do you mean by that exactly?'

'Well Brad, since you ask, it means no potential experience will be avoided, ignored or sidelined if it in someway contributes to my art.

D. approaches us dressed in what is best described as vintage porn. 'Hello boys,' she says.

'Well hello,' I say, 'you're looking very Bettie page, November 1958. And it's been raining for six straight days and you haven't left your room, which is situated in a bad part of town. You want company and strong liquor. Shall I go on?'

'You've sold me honey,' she drawls, 'you've got me smoldering, I'm hot and in need of quenching.'

'D,' says Brad, 'I don't think this is wise. Think of your image. This man is a ne'er do well, a fop, a boulevardier, an...' Brad swallows, '...an artist

'Exactly what I'm looking for,' says D. taking my proffered hand.

Brad, I notice, has taken out his Blackberry and is tapping it frantically with two fingers, like a blind organist wearing sunglasses at midnight mass in a blackout trying to hammer out Ave Maria.

We push past him and walk onto Leicester Square and hail a taxi.

Excerpts from an Artist's (so-called) life...

Adult material

'Where to squire?' The cabbie looks at us with a double take as we climb into the back.

'Take us to the cheapest, sleaziest hotel in Paddington via a Londis.'

Having bought four bottles of Jack Daniels and two packs of schmokes we roll up outside the Arcadia, a doss house of a hotel, patronised by prostitutes and traveling salesmen.

'What you want?' a receptionist asks in an accent that's a blend of Eastern European and Cockney. You'd believe she was on a gap year if it wasn't for the tattoos. She was more likely recruiting runaways for Russian crime controlled prostitution rings.

'Listen sister,' I say, 'we want a room for the night, with a view of the street and close to the neon Arcadia sign so we can hear it buzzing. There's an extra 20 clams in it for you if you don't say anything to the Feds, should they come enquiring about us.' Not knowing what to make of this she nods to the board on the desk which offers the tariff: £20 per night, breakfast not included. There followed a list of services;

**Condoms, Vaseline and
specialist room service visits
to suit everyone's desires.
Discretion our byword.
Inquire at reception for prices.**

Handing over two perfectly folded £20 notes we carried our Londis bags of alcohol and schmokes to room 36. Opening the window onto the street with its view over Paddington Station, we notice a faint buzz emanating from the sign. The pavement was littered with nine or ten street lunatics drinking cider and arguing with themselves and each other.

D., having poured two measures of JD into matching tea cups, slowly and methodically begins to undress. I light two Marlboros as she drops her bra over the red bedside lamp. Dressed in a black thong and stockings with 8" stiletto's, she hands me a cup, swapping it for a schmoke, and lies supine on the bed. Taking a gulp and reaching for the bottle I refill our cups saying, 'I'm not sure whether to spank you or draw you?'

'Your choice Jonny,' she leers, 'though my preference is the former. I've been bad Jonny, very bad. I need the badness spanked out of me.'

I flip my cigarette through the open window, take off my light sienna with a white chalk stripe linen jacket, placing it over the back of a chair and roll-up my shirt sleeves. D. gasps. 'Turn over.' I command. She gasps again. 'Push your bum in the air,' now she starts to moan. 'Six!' I say out loud. D. faints.

In the 40 minutes that D. is out I take a pad of Bristol board and a black Pentel brush pen from my satchel and complete six illustrations.

I've just placed an order for Chinese food, off a menu card I found by the phone, and I'm slugging from a bottle of JD. as D. wakes.

Crawling out of the bed and pulling herself up by climbing my legs, she rests her head on my shoulder, looks at the bed, looks at the drawings, looks at me, looks back at the bed and says, 'that was fucking brilliant! It's true what they say about you.'

'What's that doll? What do they say?'

'That you're an experience.'

'Yes D. Yes I am.'

As D. raises a bottle of JD. to her lips there's a rap on the door. 'It's either a hit or our takeaway food,' I say. Opening the door the length of the chain, I look through the gap at a geezer in a crash helmet with his arms full of takeaway boxes. Reaching under my jacket for reassurance, I slip the chain off.

'Mr Marlowe?'

'Yes.' I say.

'I have your order.'

'Bring it in, let me pour you a drink.'

Man, for that is his name, fills a papercup and helps himself to a schmoke. 'You're Deviant Vivika,' he says glancing over at the bed.

'You're right,' she says.

'And you're that artist who paints...'

'Yep! I interject. 'And you're more than a deliveryman.'

'True. I moonlight this job to meet interesting people.'

'Why?' asks D.

'To offer them an invite and assured admittance to The Club.'

'The Club?' I ask.

'The Hellfire Club. I'm the doorman and I alone decide who shall or shall not enter.'

'Sold.' says D.

'In that case, count me in,' I say.

Draining his cup and dropping his cigarette butt into it, Man opens the door and, stepping into the corridor says, 'be seeing you,' as he's enveloped in the darkness of the stairwell.

'What the fuck! He didn't tell us where to go,' pouts D. who's clearly up for further adventures.

'Let's eat,' I say, snapping chopsticks and opening cartons of hot food.

Slurping and draining our cartons to the last noodle and still feeling peckish our eyes fall on a solitary Fortune Cookie. Being the gentleman I have no recourse but to offer it to D.

D. taking the cookie, breaks it in half and gives me the paper fortune.

'Fuck me!' I exclaim.

'What?' says D. picking crumbs off her breasts and leaning over.

'It says:

1am. 16B Karswell Street. W1.

I think this is our invite. Get dressed D.'

Excerpts from an Artist's (so-called) life...

Hell Yes!

Hailing a taxi outside the hotel we ask the driver to take us to Karswell Street.

'Well I'll be, in 40 years driving, I've never dropped anyone there. This'll be a first,' says the cabbie.

'Where is it?' I ask.

'Just off Baker Street. I think it's a private road, still cobbled, still has gas lamps. Victorian mansions. It's somewhere all the cabbies know but no one admits to having been there. This'll be one to tell the lads, if they believe me.'

Ten minutes later we were driving down Baker Street.

'Next on the right,' says the cabbie indicating and pulling over. 'I don't think we're able to drive down there.'

Looking through the cab window, I can see outlined by the headlights black steel gates, similar to those outside of Downing Street. D.V. Who's been dozing, shakes herself awake, plumps her breasts, grabs my hand and says, 'let's go!'

I hand the driver a perfectly folded £20 note with a request to 'keep the change.'

As the taxi turns to go back the way it came, we walk a dozen steps to the gates. A figure in a top hat and tails walks out from behind a tree and says to us through the gate, 'what is your business here sir?'

'We have an invite to The Hellfire Club.'

'Ah! You are D. and your female companion is D.V. We are expecting you.' Turning a key he holds the gate open saying, 'it's the 5th house down on the right.'

We walk past grandiose Gothic properties with glimmers of light barely escaping through heavily curtained windows until we reach 16B. Walking up a steep set of marble steps to the front door we ring the bell and, fuck me, if an owl didn't hoot at the same time and what sounded like a wolf, howl. It was like a scene from a Hammer horror film.

'I love it!'

D. was clearly impressed. The door opened and Man, dressed all in black, bade us welcome. 'Listen,' he said, 'the children of the night, what music they make.' A broad smile widened on his face. A Man with a sense of humour.

'My kinda place,' said D. stepping into the hallway, Man's reference going completely over her head.

'The show's just about to start, follow me to your table.' Man led us down a corridor into a drawing room, studded with intimate two person tables and chairs. In the middle of each table was a burning red candle. Eight tables, eight couples and the glow from each candle throwing a subdued light onto a stage. Opening a bottle of Chateauneuf Du Pape 1990 and pouring two glasses, he whispers, 'did I mention the price for this evening's entertainment? No? It is participation. Yes!' And disappears into the dark.

There is a click and a spotlight from behind our heads lights up a figure standing on the stage.

Excerpts from an Artist's (so-called) life...

Kabaret

'Ladies and Gentlemen. Fellow worshipers at the alter of the profane.
Allow me to introduce our opening act.
All the way from the foot of Mount Doom. They endured an excruciating painful journey along the River Styx and fought their way across the Bridge of Sighs to be with you tonight.

'I, Lucifer, present:
'The Dwarfs from Hell.'
Let the screams Begin!'

The spotlight dims for a second, the MC vanishes and is replaced by seven dwarfs on a unicycle juggling flaming rabbits. D. gasps as do many in the audience. I count six rabbits being flambéed. 'This is more interesting than pulling rabbits out of a hat,' I say to D.
'Look over there!' She says pointing to an eighth dwarf with a telescopic rifle on top of a bookcase in a far corner of the room.
I reach for my mock Glock. There is a sudden BANG! And one of the dwarfs on the unicycle spins and falls to the stage, blood pouring from a sucking chest wound.

Two more bangs, and two more dead dwarfs. D. mesmerized breathes, 'this is incredible.'

I count six flaming rabbits being juggled by three, BANG!, two, BANG!, one dwarf. Juggling six flaming rabbits and peddling a unicycle in figure 8s proves too much for the remaining dwarf who crashes onto the stage. The rabbits all land on top of him setting him ablaze. The dwarf shooter jumping from the bookcase throws himself on top of the burning pyre. There is a smell of chicken in the air and I'm suddenly hungry. Spontaneous applause erupts, D. shouts, 'Encore!'

'Wishful thinking,' I think. The light blinks out and on again, the smoldering corpses have been replaced by the MC. Lucifer, for it is he, illuminated by a flaming rabbit on a silver platter held up by Man.

'Life is a kabaret, only a Kabaret and I love a kabaret! Tonite is very special! After making headlines at his war crimes trial at the Hague, this is his second only appearance in a country he is not a despot of. I, Lucifer bring you, courtesy of the UN, Interpol and Her Majesty's Secret Service, Vlad Smythz, former dictator of a small Eastern European country, now a stand-up comedian.

Wanted for crimes against humanity by governments across the free world Vlad makes his debut here tonite, please put your hands together and give a warm welcome to Vlaaaaaaaaad Smythz!'

Escorted into the room by a phalanx of armed guards, a small man in a military uniform and peaked cap goose steps onto the stage.

Excerpts from an Artist's (so-called) life...

Former prison bitch

D. is enthralled. Vlad salutes the room to hisses from the audience. Slapping his chest with a fist he says, 'What good is sitting alone in your room? I know where you live. I will kill you in more ways than you know how to die. You! Laugh. I command you!' Pointing to a couple he says, 'You! How do you want to be disposed of?' Taking a glass of wine off the table he holds it up proclaiming, 'This glass of wine will be mine and be hailed as revolutionary!'

Pointing with a leather gloved hand and in a staccato rant, Vlad screams at the audience, 'You! You want a blindfold with that cigarette? You! Laugh now. Tomorrow you won't be laughing! You! When I say there is only one way. It is my way! Some call me an evil genius, some an egomaniacal dictator. You! My minions, may call me Your Excellency. And all that I ask is blind obedience. You! You ask me who am I afraid of? You? I tell you no one! Although, come to think of it, Keyser Söze terrifies me. You? You may call me El Presidente!'

Someone in the audience calls out, 'You! You need to be medicated.'

An incensed Vlad straight arm salutes the audience. 'You! If I give you the finger, it's telling you how many seconds you have left to live.'

D. applauds and stands up shouting, 'Vlad, you put the fun into fundamentalism!' Turning to me she says, 'I've been bad Dave. Very bad!'

From the stage Vlad clicks his heels together and spitting addresses the audience. 'You! You will know my wrath. Nothing will spare you from my revenge! Laugh! I command you. I will crush my enemies! I will wipe them from the face of the map! I will snatch this defeat from the jaws of freedom! You will fruitlessly battle to get me from this stage!'

At this point a dozen armed guards in riot gear enter the room and drag Vlad from the stage. Breaking away he rushes back onto the stage shouting, 'What I demand is total! You will thank me on bended knees!' Four guards with riot shields kettle Vlad towards an exit. Passing our table he points at me and shouts, 'You! You want a last cigarette?' And with a final cry of, 'Laugh! I command you!' Vlad is bundled from the room.

Jumping back to her feet D. applauds and begins to throw items of clothing at the now locked door. 'This is theatre Dave, pure kabaret. Bravo! Encore! I'll get Brad to open negotiations with the International War Crimes Tribunal, see if we can't book him. God I feel dirty Dave. I'm so bad. I need discipline Dave.'

As I'm working out a scenario for D. and me, the spotlight goes out and immediately comes back on again, shining on the stage. Stepping into the light the MC fingering a Daliesque mustache says, 'Rumours that the UN are sending in a Piss Taking Force are not actually true. Vlad Smythz will return later in the year. And now the third and final act in tonites show. I, Lucifer present Audience participation. This is the price you pay for admittance to The Hellfire Club. The thud of four spotlights being switched on catches the attention, as they light up four doors in different corners of the room.

Excerpts from an Artist's (so-called) life...

Behind door number one

'Ladies, Gentlemen and Deviants, I, Lucifer will make your fantasies a reality. All except you,' he says pointing a long nailed finger at me, 'there is nothing I can offer you that you haven't experienced. The price of admission is participation and all, except you Dave, are invited through the doors. Once you enter there is no return, only you, Dave, may egress the way you entered. You will notice on each door a metal plate, touch it and the door will open. Your choices are Pleasure and Pain; Medieval Dungeon; An audience with Nick Clegg and Disneyland. Your choice, your responsibility, the consequences yours alone.'

D. kissing me on the cheek, gets up saying 'I've been bad Dave, it's the Medieval Dungeon for me. Later.'

Man appears at my side. 'Allow me to show you out.' Reaching the door Man says, 'incidentally Mr L. says don't forget to invite him to your opening.'

Excerpts from an Artist's (so-called) life...

Deviant Vivika and the Medieval Dungeon ©

[Editor's Note: Again due to the explicit nature of this excerpt the decision to withhold publication has been taken.]

Excerpts from an Artist's (so-called) life...

It's all in the mind

Finding myself on Baker Street, the sun beginning to light up the buildings, I take a leisurely perambulation to my gaff in Soho. Stepping over M. I let myself in, enter and exit the shower and flop onto the bed. I wake 24hours later. 'Breakfast in Bar Italia,' I think. Slipping a perfectly folded £10 note into M's pocket, I notice a headline on page three of the Metro covering him;

'Deviant Vivika Missing.

Last seen in the company of a so-called contemporary artist, see Brian Sewell pg. 10, 11, 12, and 14. Brad Powers, spokesperson for Ms Vivika said, 'D. is taking a well earned break and will inform us of her whereabouts when she is ready. The police are not involved. Thank you.'

A couple of minutes later I'm sitting at a table in Bar Italia drinking espresso doppios with a plateful of pain au chocolat and tapping the Metro's number on my cell phone. 'Put me through to your arts correspondent.' Ms Metro answers. 'Hi,' I say.
'Dave Hi! It's about D. isn't it?'
'Yep.'

'Apparently she checked out of a rehab clinic this morning and is currently holed up in a hotel somewhere. Although I don't believe any of it. Probably a publicity stunt timed to coincide with the launch of her CD of Marc Almond covers. But I do know SoWhat! Magazine are featuring her in the new issue.'

'Fanx,' I say, 'and when you see Alan tell him I'll go with him to West London.' Finishing my coffee, I leave a perfectly folded £10 note under my plate and with a flourish and a 'Ciao Fabio,' I walk out onto Frith Street.

Speed dialing DS. at SoWhat! Magazine, I suggest she meets me for a lunchtime drink at the Soho Hotel at. She agrees immediately and promises to bring a copy of the new issue before it hits the streets.

Excerpts from an Artist's (so-called) life...

Nothing to write home about

'Is any of this actually true?' I ask D. at the same time reading the cover blurb for the new issue:

'Exclusive! Is it over for Deviant Vivika?
As she checks into rehab we ask
'Is contemporary art to blame?
Did Deviant Vivika secretly marry artist
after posing for him?'
Full story inside.

I open the magazine and on page 4, under Deborah Slurs' picture and byline it reads:

'SoWhat! can exclusively reveal that within days of trying to crucify herself, Deviant 'I am the Antichrist, give me a baby!' Vivika swung from suicidal to matrimonial, proposing to anyone with a pulse.

We can now report that the unhinged beauty checked in and out of rehab like a deranged yo-yo. Close friends say that when she tried to kill herself it was less of a plea for help, more a cry for room service.

She has repeatedly been photographed knickerless on wild nights out and checks herself into sleazy hotels under assumed names.

Only days ago she threatened to kill herself by gulping down three industrial sized bottles of painkillers. She held up the bottles of Co-codamol and shouted, 'I'm gonna do this. This is it! I'm through with the whole fucking circus!'

Close friends of close friends of the family are remaining tight lipped, although an acquaintance of a friend said, 'It's that artist innit. What's his name, the bloke who paints those naked women, that led her astray.'

Brad Powers spokesperson for Deviant Vivika said, 'Deviant Vivika will be signing copies of her new CD 'The Torch Songs of Marc Almond' at 12noon on Friday at HMV Oxford Street.'

'I think it answers my question. It's all bollocks.'

'But it sells copies Dave.' And as Brad said to me, 'Any press is good press.'

'Deborah?'

'Yes Dave.'

'There's a club I want to take you to and in it there's a room I'll introduce you to. You may be in there some time.'

'Love to Dave. Bell me. Also, don't forget to find time to paint me for the exhibition.'

'Fuck me! Unbelievable!' I think getting up. 'Going for a pee,' I say, walking across the lobby. Slipping the bathroom attendant a perfectly folded £10 note, I say, pointing to DS, 'call security, there's a so-called journalist waiting to shove a microphone into Chelsy's face when she arrives for lunch.' I then climb out of the bathroom window.

Excerpts from an Artist's (so-called) life...

Gonzo artist

We were somewhere around Heathrow on the edge of the airport when the drugs began to take hold. I remember Alan saying something like, 'I'll pick you up in the morning, I'm going to see my dealer.' And suddenly there was a terrible roar as a plane zoomed over our heads and the sky was full of what looked like an Anish Kapoor sculpture. And Alan was driving about a 100 miles an hour. And a voice was screaming...

'What the fuck! Where am I, goddamn it!' I then recognised my own voice. 'Are we there yet? Are we there yet? Are we goddamn there yet?' I was beginning to panic, paranoid that the Federales were going to pull us over. Schmoking a Wandsworth Wonder and with his head leaning out of the window, Alan drove into a Tesco customer carpark at 75mph, screeched into a handbrake turn by the recycling dumpsters, handed over a brown envelope to a dodgy looking geezer, who in turn handed him a brown package, and zoomed back out of the carpark in the direction of Central London. And at no time did the car drop below 30mph.

Turning to me he says, 'I'm having those bottle banks at the weekend.' And passes me the remains of the 2Ws.

45 minutes later we're sitting in the Coach and Horses in Soho and I've got the munchies. 'Fucking PR motherfuckers,' I say to no one in particular.

'Word!' Says N.C. at the next table.

'What are you doing here, man?' says Alan, 'incidentally this is my mate Dave...'

'Yeah! Man, I recognise you from the Observer. You guys free this PM?'

'Yep! Why do you ask?'

'My sister wants a painting of herself for the wall of her new apartment. She's having a housewarming tonight, why don't you guys come? And if you're free now, I'm shooting a scene for my forthcoming film, 'Shaft Rules yer Momma.©' A homage to 70s blaxploitation movies.

'You mean Shaft?'

'Ya damn right!'

'Shaft!'

'Can you dig it?'

'Shaft!'

'Right On!'

'They say Shaft is a bad mother..!'

'Shut your mouth!'

'You're talking about Shaft!'

'We can dig it!'

'Nigel Shaft!'

Alan pauses between sips of his pint, considers this for a moment and says, 'NIGEL fucking Shaft! Do me a favour.'

I pause for a second from stuffing black pepper and sea salt cashews into my mouth and say, 'NIGEL goddamn Shaft! You're taking a fucking liberty. Who's funding this travesty? The children's channel?'

'Since you ask. Yes.'

'Where's your goddamn integrity?' Alan asks.

'Better still,' I say, 'where's the goddamn catering truck? I'll need a full stomach if I'm going to stand around as an extra for the next couple of hours, regardless of what you're paying me. Which begs the question. What are you paying me?'

'£200 for three hours work.'

'I'm in,' says Alan, draining his pint.

Excerpts from an Artist's (so-called) life...

Are you talking to me?

We're standing in St. Anne's Court, which has been cordoned off to allow filming to take place. I'm in a crowd of bystanders who get caught up in a stand-off between Nigel Shaft and three pimps, who are trading in underage young people for work in sweat shops, sex shops and drug drops.

'Action!' shouts N.C.

'Say! Homes, what's happenin? Where you at?' Says the actor playing Shaft.

'What you say homes? We all live here. This is our homes, homes.'

'I'm here to bring you down. You bad people. Bringing drugs into people's homes, homes.'

Reaching breaking point. I snap. 'Who the fuck wrote this crap?'

N.C. Cries, 'Cut!'

There's a general call for, 'Quiet on the set!' 'Have some respect people,' and, 'He's got a point.'

Leaving the set an hour later, and £200 better off, Alan and I decide to return to the Coach and Horses and pick-up where we left off.

'Four pints of London Pride and er...four more pints please.' Alan, sitting back down, says 'I'll tell you Dave, this schmoking ban is making me drink more.'

Failing to see the logic and not caring much either way, I drink my pints while Alan rings for a mini-cab to take us to Camden.

'Apparently Ns. sister is 26 and has just moved into a new place by the Market. Also, N. tells me, she's a great admirer of your work and wants to be painted by you.'

'I'll see what I can do.' I say.

Having drained the last of our beers, I hand the barman a perfectly folded £50 note with a request to, 'be lucky.'

Climbing into the back of the mini-cab we sit back and wait. 'When you're ready,' says Alan, who appears a little tense.

'Ready for what?' says the driver.

'To take us to Camden Market.'

'Where's that?'

'Where's what?'

'Camden Market.'

'Camden.'

'Camden. Where's that?'

Alan clenches his fists, and I'm sure he's going to punch the driver, but instead takes a deep breath. 'Let me get this straight,' he says, breathing out slowly, 'this is a mini-cab?'

'Yeah!'

'You're a mini-cab driver, and you take people to destinations they request?'

'Yeah!'

'Good. Turn the engine on and take us to Camden Market.'

'A market won't be open this time of night.'

'This is not a discussion.' Alan says beginning to lose his composure. 'Take us to Camden.'

'Where's that?'

Alan's Zen state of oneness was rapidly turning into a state of psychosis.

Grabbing my hand to keep calm, he says, 'how long have you been a mini-cab driver?'

'bout 20 minutes.'

'What were you doing before this?'

'Four years unemployed, mate. They give you any job to get you off the dole. It's good for the government's statistics, innit?'

Alan's beginning to mellow. 'Tell you what,' he says, 'you just drive and we'll give you directions.'

Looking in the rear view mirror at us, he says, 'slight problem with that.'

'What's that?' asks Alan.

'Can't drive!'

'Okay! Here's the plan.' Says Alan. 'I'll drive, you, what's your name geezer?'

'Tom.'

'You, Tom, sit in the back with Dave. Let's party! And. Before I forget, I get to keep the cab as my latest found sculpture.'

Tom, somewhat nonplussed nods in agreement.

Excerpts from an Artist's (so-called) life...

Fun for all ages

Arriving in Camden we make our way to what was once a bicycle factory but is   now luxury apartments. Ringing the bell N.C. lets us in with a warm, 'Dudes! Welcome. Let me introduce you to my sister, you know of her, but you haven't met her. Sheila. This is Alan and Dave. Alan and Dave meet Sheila.'

'Well! So you're Dave. Pleased to meetcha.'

Totally ignoring Alan, she grabs me by the arm and heads into an open plan living room with panoramic views over London. 'Nice vista,' I say, helping myself to a plate of canapés and a bottle of wine. 'So Sheila, what can you do for me?'

'Come with me,' she says, 'I've something to show you.'

Following her across the living room I take in the 70s décor, with a 70s soundtrack CD playing in the background. I also notice the lack of guests. Drinking the wine and grabbing a tray of vol-au-vents, I ask, 'Are we early?'

'Come in,' she opens the door to her bedroom. 'You're are my only guest.'

The bedroom is completely decorated in leopard print wallpaper and the ceiling is mirrored. In the centre of the room is an oversize round bed covered in a leopard print plush material, and hanging over it a leopard skin wrapped trapeze.

Taking off her dress in one yank and kicking of her shoes, she reclines on the bed wearing leopard print underwear. 'Dave,' she purrs, 'they tell me you always sleep with your models. Well, take me I'm yours, and then paint me and hang me in your new exhibition.'

Popping the last prawn vol-au-vent into my mouth, I say, 'loo?'

'Meow!' she says pointing to a door on the other side of the bedroom.

'Back in a mo.' I say edging around the bed. Locking the door behind me and turning on the shower, I ring Alan from my cell phone and arrange to meet him outside. I then climb out of the bathroom window.

Excerpts from an Artist's (so-called) life...

Not a serving suggestion

Rendezvousing with Alan on the street, he gives me a knowing look and says, 'bathroom window?'

'Yep! And, would you agree, brother and sister. Barking?'

'Yep!'

'At least it's given us time to get to the flash-mob graffiti event on Waterloo Bridge. Where's the mini-cab?'

'In the car park under the apartments. Follow me.' Alan strides out purposefully. 'By the way,' he says taking a claw hammer and 8" screwdriver from out of his jacket, 'I'm having the 'Max Headroom 10m' sign for my collection.

Ten minutes later sliding the sign into the cab, we drive off in the direction of the South Bank. All we know about tonight's situation is a text we each received informing us of the time and location. The word on the street is that a group of graffiti artists are flying in to drive-by graffiti Waterloo Bridge. Parking in Stamford Street we walk up to the centre of the bridge, mingling with 500 or so flash-mobbers.

From the crowd there's a shout of, 'Dave!' And guerrilla graffiti artist Wanksta walks out of the crowd towards us, his look-out Vincenzo at his side.

Alan immediately asks, 'who are they and where are they from?'

'Apparently,' says Wanksta, 'they're a Neasden art collective, their work borrowing heavily from the Russian scatological group 'Voina.'

'I'm bored already,' I say.

'Give them a chance,' says Wanksta, who, looking over my shoulder, points to three fuckwits in hoodies handing out flyers.

Grabbing a handful Vincenzo snorts, 'wankers!'

Alan grins, says 'Hey. We all started out naive.'

'Hell yes!' replies Wanksta.

'Hell no!' I say, picking up a discarded flyer which reads:

**'Welcome to the Waterloo Bridge Graffiti Event.
A two finger sign to the police and our 'rents.
Graffiti rules innit.
We shall return.'**

At the bottom of the flyer there is a list of 'phone numbers and email addresses. 'Vincenzo you called it,' I say balling the flyer and lobbing into the Thames. Two of the three aspiring graffiti artists have now unpacked their backpacks and taken out five cans of Holt's car spray paint. The third hoodie is watching for signs of the Old Bill.

Wanksta yawns. 'There's four community plods walking towards us from the Strand. Two Old Bill on either side of the road coming at us from Waterloo, and the guy with a beard and the camera is an undercover Old Bill. He, you will notice, appears to be talking to himself. He's probably coordinating the arrests.'

Everyone in the crowd watches as a hoodie sprays a badly drawn penis shooting cum over two circles which, I believe, are meant to represent breasts. At this point the crowd, as bored as I am, turns to leave.

A police van slowly comes to a stop by the hoodies who are now standing back admiring their work. The three of them, noticing the van, decide to leg it in opposite directions, and run straight into the arms of the approaching Old Bill who, it should be said, are looking as bored as I feel.

'If only Robin would stop encouraging it,' says Wanksta.

'I'm off, I've got a date with Ms Metro,' says Alan walking in the direction of Stamford Street. 'And don't forget to bell me when the Former Dictator makes his return.'

'We've gotta go too,' Wanksta nods in the direction of Vincenzo. 'It's our Hippocratic duty to spray, 'Life is Short, Art is Long,' on the Thames side of Blackfriers Bridge. Vincenzo's going to hold me upside down by the ankles. Let me know about the Vlad gig.'

'Me too,' says Vincenzo, 'Ciao!'

I decide to walk to Soho.

Excerpts from an Artist's (so-called) life...

Today's top story

Lying on my chaise lounge, sipping a Campari and soda, squeaky after my 55 minute shower, I switch on Sky News while I wait for my Carluccio's takeaway delivery. On screen is Brad Powers, PR consultant to Deviant Vivika, being interviewed about Former Dictator Vlad Smythz.

'Yes I can confirm,' he says, 'that Ms Vivika's company and Louie Cypher productions© are standing surety for...'

' A former despot?' asks the reporter.

'Mr Smythz,' continues Brad, 'will be on day release and perform a community service through the medium of entertainment.'

'Why would the International War Crimes Tribunal allow the release of a man of Vlad Smythz' reputation. A reputation earned through his his neo-fascist views and his government sanctioned practice of torture, false imprisonment and the disappearance of political opponents and ordinary citizens with alternate political views. With over 3000 deaths on his hands...'

'Alleged deaths,' interrupts Brad, 'no-one has yet said how those mass graves got there or who dug them.'

'Mr Powers are you insane?'

The screen goes black for a second and the studio anchor apologies for the break in transmission. Touching her ear she says, 'we're going back to Tim at the Hague.'

'I apologise for any insult to you.'

'None taken,' smiles Brad. 'With the cooperation of Louie Cypher productions© we intend to show another side to Vlad Smythz.'

'One can tell you're a public relations executive,' says the now red faced reporter.

'What we're supporting,' continues Brad, 'is Art! His appearances will be performance pieces. Conceptual art, if you will.'

'ART!' shouts the reporter.

Someone off camera can be heard whispering, 'Tim! Calm down Tim.'

'We're submitting him for the Turner Prize and he'll have his own section in the international Pavilion at the Venice Biennale.' Brad shows the camera a smug white-toothed grin.

'I cannot believe...you're radio rental!' says the reporter as he advances threateningly towards Brad. 'You PR mother...' The sound is abruptly cut off as two production crew wrestle him to the ground.

There's a Ding Dong! And I zap the 56" wide screen HD Matt black TV into oblivion. Opening the door I'm greeted by a courier holding three, four course meals, four bottles of Soavé and a kilo of Italian roast 100% Arabica coffee. Tipping the geezer a perfectly folded £20 note, I take the food.

As the the courier turns to leave he says, 'Did you know there's a guy sleeping on your doorstep?'

'Yes.' I say. 'Yes I do.' Shaking the snoring M. by the shoulder, I say as his eyes begin to focus on me, 'Martin time for a shower before dinner.'

M. spends twenty minutes in the shower, punctuating the splashing with the occasional shout of 'Harold!' Wearing one of my white linen Polo shirts and Ralph Lauren black linen trousers, Martin sits down at the table and tucks into the antipasta.

Forty minutes later, we've eaten all the food and are drinking the last of the wine when an idea occurs to me.

Excerpts from an Artist's (so-called) life...

For promotional use only

'Warhol did it, why shouldn't I?' I say out loud.

Martin looks at me blankly, 'What did Warhol do?'

'Funny you should ask Martin. Funny you should ask. Tomorrow afternoon I'm supposed to be interviewed at the ICA. Part of a series of face to face talks with artists about their work. The event is programmed as 'The Evolution of the Nude in 20th Century Art.' There is a 45 minute interview followed by 15-20 minutes of questions from the audience. And you Martin will be standing in for me for the afternoon.'

Martin looks at me, shouts. 'Harold!' and then calmly says, 'I think Dave. That I am. Your man.'

'Okay,' I say, 'here's the plan. The fee they give you on arrival is yours. Pick yourself a linen suit out of the closet and anything else you need. The top drawer of the dressing table is full of Raybans, take a pair and don't take them off. And there's only one proviso.'

'That is?'

'I'm glad you asked Martin. I'm glad you asked. When you leave, you must exit through the toilet window.'

Excerpts from an Artist's (so-called) life...

Thank you! Thank you!

Excerpts from the reviews:

The ICA played host to a unique artist's talk last night when contemporary artist Dave lectured the audience on the nude in 20th century art by arguing the similarities inherent, using the analogy of the rag and bone business through to contemporary recycling. His premise being that the nude is infinitely used and reused and is traded like any commodity. He went on to answer questions from the audience with shouts of 'Harold.'
Although the argument on a superficial level made a case for the use and reuse of the nude in art, the event was more a performance piece than a treatise. The Guardian.

'Absolute nonsense. Another example of the vacuity of modern art. And who, may I ask, is Harold?' B. Sewell. Evening Standard.

Dave, looking every inch a cool dude, dressed in linen and Raybans seduced an ICA audience of note-takers, piss-takers and muck-rakers.
Answering obtuse questions about the nude and its relationship to obscure French philosophers with cries of 'Harold!' Dave once again illustrates the inseparability of art and artist. Metro

As this arts correspondent can attest, having followed the career of Dave, art and artist are one. And never more so than last night's lecture at the ICA.

As goatee bearded intellectuals asked questions referencing Rive Gauche philosophers, and, in my opinion, missing the points being made apropos the recycling of the female form in art.

Dave subsequently stunned them with the retort 'Harold!' Leaving many in the audience stroking their chins and looking non-plussed, and he himself leaving via the restroom window. Susie Smith. Fork It!©

As the forthcoming exhibition will attest, the nude in art is as relevant today as it's always been. And I'm proud to participate in this tradition by posing for Dave for his exhibition.

I've been Deborah Slur. SoWhat! Magazine.

Excerpts from an Artist's (so-called) life...

Never read the label

10pm. Thursday. Soho Theatre. Dean Street. W1

Billed as a one-off performance piece by Former Dictator Vlad Smythz, the bar is full of artists, largests and alarmists all wanting a piece of the action.

SoWhat! Magazine described the event in their usual hyperbole as a 'once in a lifetime experience.'

BS. in the Standard wrote a long piece attacking the shock tactics involved, calling it 'Trite, passé and 'an affront to common decency.' A charge picked-up by the Daily Mail who guaranteed through their vitriolic editorial attacks a full house for tonight's show

Westminster Council's 11th hour attempt to close down the performance failed after Brad Powers' presentation to the High Court arguing freedom of speech.

'What about freedom of speech for his victims?' I say to Alan returning from the bar with 30 bottles of Becks. Handing five bottles each to Ms. Metro, Wanksta©, Vincenzo and his boyfriend Nine Mil Phil©, I take mine and offer up a toast, 'Oh Art! What atrocities are committed in thy name?'

There is a collective cry of 'ART' and the clinking of bottles coinciding with a request to 'take your seats for tonight's performance.'

We take our balcony seats as the lights dim and a spotlight illuminates a figure standing on the stage. There is a hush. A quiet. A sound of silence that drowns out the screams of the dead.

'Perhaps Brian is right,' I say to Alan, who looks at me putting a finger to his lips as the MC taps the head of a microphone.

'Ladies and Gentlemen!
What good is sitting alone in your room?
You haven't come here to pray.
Life is a kabaret, my Stalin
You're here for the kabaret.

Put down the AK 47
The IED and the whip
Time for a holiday.
Life is a kabaret, my Satan
You're here for the kabaret.

I, Lucifer, bring you the return of Former Dictator Vlad Smythz. I thank you! I thank you! No. I thank you! No really! I thank you!

The lights go down and there is a slight smell of fireworks, as six heavily armed guards push a gurney onto the stage. Unstrapping Vlad Smythz, dressed in an orange jumpsuit, they chain him to a heavy metal ring set into the stage and take their seats in the front row.

Vlad coughs and, addressing the audience, says, 'If you see me watching you from dark alleys and 4th floor windows, if you should catch a glimpse of me from behind a tree, know this, your death is certain at this point.'

Pointing to a couple who are tutting, he says, 'You! You want a piece of me? Stand in line. But know this, the only line I stand in is in the line of fire.'

Ms. Metro leans over the balcony and shouts, 'Just who do you think you are?'

Vlad looks up, slams a clenched fist into his chest and says, 'My name? My name is Vlad Smythz! I deliver stand-up comedy with menaces!' He points to the guards exclaiming, 'You! Laugh I command you!'

Someone shouts out, 'Pick fruit, not fights!'

Vlad counters with, Is that all you got you muppet?'

There is a murmured, 'Fucker's a dial-tone.'

An incensed Vlad, spittle sliding down his chin, steam rising from his head in the heat of the spotlights, clicks his heels together, like a homicidal Dorothy, and screams at the audience, 'Who wants some?'

There are cries of, 'Fuck off!' from around the auditorium. Someone shouts, 'You're a Public Relations conceived, one dimensional joke. An insult to the Avant-Garde. I didn't give my art to Dada to participate in this goddamn travesty.' I realise that it's me haranguing Vlad and start to climb over the balcony. Wanksta© and Vincenzo grab me by the shoulders and push me back into my seat. Alan takes a full bottle of Becks off me as I'm about to launch it at Vlad's head. Nine Mil Phil© taking the bottle throws it, dead straight at the stage. Time slows and I watch its progress as it arcs towards Vlad. There is a loud, 'ZANG!' as the bottle hits the microphone in front of Vlad's throat and zings off stage left.

Vlad, looking a little shocked, stands up straight, holds his arms out at each side, rests his head on one shoulder and, addressing the audience, says. 'My public! Why has thou forsaken me?'

I hear myself shouting, 'Defenestrate the motherfucker!' to applause from the audience.

Vlad strains against his chains, points up at me and says, 'It's a conspiracy. A plot against me. Me! Vlad Smythz. Well let me tell you, I have a plot for you and it's big enough for the rest of you poseurs.'

There is a collective gasp as the realisation of Vlad's remark hits home. Bottles, handbags, pens, iphones, lipsticks, a dwarf, rain down on Vlad.

'Now this is more like it,' says Alan.

'This is better than naked men running through the audience, although not as pretentious,' says Ms Metro making notes.

The stage meanwhile is surrounded by armed guards. Vlad, gripping the microphone shouts, 'Call in an airstrike! Kill them! Kill them all!' Straight arm saluting the audience he rants, 'You! You want a last cigarette? You! Laugh I command you!'

As they escort him from the stage the last thing out of his mouth is a shout of, 'I will have my revenge!'

The lights flicker and a figure rises up from the stage. 'Ladies, Gentlemen and Situationalists. I,Lucifer, thank you for you participation in tonight's performance, Former Dictator Vlad Smythz will return. He his currently appearing at the Hague, courtesy of the UN, standing room only.'

There is a flash and the stage is empty. 'Bored now,' I say, 'the Groucho?'

There is a collective, 'Yeah!'

Excerpts from an Artist's (so-called) life...

Power to the People

As we exit onto Dean Street the Met's anti-riot squads are trying to stop Vlad's security vehicle from being turned over.

The Old Bill are starting to kettle the protesters as we slip through the cordon. Walking towards the Groucho, Wanksta© sprays a yellow smiley face on a stationary police car and throwing the spray can to Vincenzo, who in turn throws back a can of green, he then sprays a Kermit face on the drivers' side window.

'Muppets!,' says Nine Mil Phil©.

Two minutes later we're sitting in the Groucho drinking Becks and vodka shots, when Ms Metro coughs and, nodding towards reception, indicates a group of Old Bill asking questions. Kate, our waitress, comes over and pretending to wipe our table, whispers 'Apparently someone graffiti'd a police car, and they believe those responsible came in here.'

'Officers!' Says Alan, 'Are you members? Has someone signed you in? Have you in fact got a warrant?'

'If not,' says Ms Metro, 'will you naff off?'

'Just who do you think you are darlin?' Says one of the Old Bill.

'I'm a reporter for the Metro newspaper. And you've outstayed your welcome.'

Noticing Wanksta's© one yellow hand and one green hand an Old Bill, pointing, says. 'Can you explain Sir, why you have paint on your hands?'

'Because I haven't washed them?'

The Old Bill ponders this for a moment, scratches his head and looking perplexed walks away leading his colleagues back onto Dean Street.

'It goes to show.' Says Alan.

'What does it show?' Asks Vincenzo.

'No idea! But then again it goes to show,' says Alan.

'What?' Says Nine Mil Phil©.

'What? What?' Says Alan.

'What goes to show?'

'It goes to show.' Alan replies swallowing a shot of vodka.

'Show what?' Asks Vincenzo.

'Who's showing?' Queries Alan.

'Dave at his one man show.' Says Wanksta©.

'How's the show coming along?' Asks Ms Metro.

I reach under my jacket and feel the warmth of the mock Glock. I feel a vein start to throb on my forehead. Taking a deep breath and slowly exhaling I say, 'It's coming along nicely,' all the while avoiding eye contact. 'In fact,' I say, 'I'm spending the day in the studio tomorrow.'

'Let's drink to that,' says Alan, signaling to our waitress, 'it's going to be a long night!'

As Kate tidies our table of empty bottles and scattered shot glasses, I climb up Vincenzo's shoulder to my feet, and stagger to the bathroom to consider my options. Climb out of the window or carry on drinking? Passing a sofa an attractive woman, with short chestnut coloured hair, catches my eye, smiles and indicates to the empty cushion next to her. I notice that she's dressed head to toe in latex. And unable to take my eyes off her I walk into the bathroom door.'

'FUCK!' I hit the floor...

...opening my eyes I see a blurred Wanksta© holding a bloodstained towel to my head.

'Whatcha Dave! Don't worry it's only a scratch!' Grabbing my hands he lifts me to my feet and, guided by Alan and Vincenzo, I return to my seat. 'What happened Dave?'

'Well Terry, to tell you the truth, in all this excitement I kind of lost track of myself.' Taking a large gulp from a bottle of Becks I notice the now empty sofa. 'Now I remember! Tall. Leggy. Latex. Great bum. Where'd she go?

'Who?' Asks Ms Metro.'

'Tall. Leggy. Latex. Great bum.' I repeat.

From behind me a husky voice with a Russian accent whispers, 'I'm here.'

We all turn around. 'Hi,' she says, and looking at me says, 'you've got to ask yourself one question. Do I feel lucky? Well do you Dave?'

I can feel everyone's eyes on me, waiting for me to say something. 'Well I'm all broke up, 'I say, 'because..?'

'Ivanka.' Says the Russian with the great bum.

'...because Ivanka and I are leaving.'

'I know what you're thinking,' says Ivanka.

'Harry Callahan.' I say.

'Dirty Harry.' Says Ivanka with a smirk.

Tipping Kate a perfectly folded £20 note and tipping my non-existent hat in the direction of the table I follow the latex clad bum onto Dean Street.

Excerpts from an Artist's (so-called) life...

A dream come true

As subtle as an Apache helicopter strike I say, 'Ivanka, you and your weapons grade latex are coming to my studio. I have paintings of you to prepare for my forthcoming show.'

Ivanka looks at me and says. 'Make me!'

'Ivanka.' I say, 'your name rhymes with a pleasure of mine, so I'd love to make you!'

Smiling she says, 'wank?'

'No darling, spank.'

'Then we have deal.'

'My studio then,' I say flagging down a taxi.

On the way to Fitzrovia I ask, 'what're you doing in London?'

'I'm with the Russian Cultural Attaché. We are sourcing art and artists to mount a joint Anglo-Russian exhibition to coincide with the 2012 Olympics. Tomorrow, or rather today, I go to Royal Academy Summer Exhibition to see what is new.'

I swallow hard. I haven't been to a RA Summer show since a panel of curators, thirdraters and masturbators rejected a painting of mine in 1998. The bitch slap of rejection was easily soothed by a private sale a week later, and I was £6000 better off. All of which, excluding 20 cases of Becks, was spent on canvases and paint for my first show six months later.

Ah! *Memories! 'Memories. Light the corners of my mind. Misty watercolour memories of..!'* I notice the cab driver looking at me in his rear view mirror. Ivanka is staring at me opened mouthed. *'...the way we were.'* I realise I'm singing out loud. Coughing I say, 'Reminiscing!'

'Barbra Streisand! Sounds a bit gay to me,' says the cabbie.

Ivanka, who's been sitting by an open window, pushes out her breasts and says, 'I assure you comrade cabbie, he is all man, but fortunately a little kinky.'

The cab driver, unable to take his eyes off Ivanka's latex enhanced nipples, mounts the pavement, scattering pedestrians every which way and, braking hard, misses a hotdog seller but slams the hotdog cart into a lamp post. Climbing nimbly from the cab we help ourselves to a couple of 'dogs, both with extra onions and mustard, and walk the rest of the way to my studio.

The hotdog vendor can be heard berating a stunned cabbie, 'It's a fucking liberty, innit?' The cabbie meanwhile is staring through the windshield at Ivanka's latex covered bum disappearing into the Soho night.

Excerpts from an Artist's (so-called) life...

Back by popular demand

Closing the doors to the cage of the elevator I push the button for the top floor. The sudden movement as it starts its climb throws Ivanka into my arms.

'Good catch comrade,' says Ivanka. Parting her Illamasqua 'Diablo' lacquered lips she proceeds to snog my face off.

Recognising the elevator is not the only thing going up, I attempt to undress Ivanka who, pausing between kisses and removing her tongue from my mouth says, 'the only way this latex dress and my black, black as Siberian night thong is coming off, is by you spanking it off.' She then thrusts her tongue back into my mouth and we continue tongue fencing. Pushing my leg between hers and grabbing her bum, I open the elevator gate and we stumble down the corridor to my studio.

Unlocking the door and falling into the open plan work space, the skylight allowing the glow from a full moon to permeate the darkness, I throw Ivanka over the paint spattered sofa. Parting her legs I peel the skin tight latex dress over her bum, exposing a perfectly rounded sphere throbbing in anticipation. I pull the black thong tight between her cheeks, she gasps releasing a sigh of pleasure.

Raising my hand I ***** **** she looks up at me and says, '***** ** ******.'

'I say, '****** **** **** and **** *** **** ***. Are you ready?'

'***** **, don't talk. I'm *** with pleasure.'

'Me too,' I say as I ***** and *****.

'More, ***** **,' says Ivanka.

I walk over to the closet, Ivanka watches my every step, you're going to ******* ****** *******,' I say taking out a ****. I ***** *** **** *** ***** **...

[Editors Note: Once again, careful editing has failed to ameliorate the explicit content of this excerpt. No censorship was or is intended. To read the longer unabridged excerpt please contact the artist directly enclosing a perfectly folded £20 note.]

Excerpts from an Artist's (so-called) life...

Based on a true story

After a night of passionate, erotic and, quite frankly, sordid sex, we breakfast on almond croissants and 100% Arabica Ethiopian coffee. I then spend the rest of the morning sketching Ivanka, using a selection of Pentel brush pens. I pose her over the paint table, under the table; on all fours; over the sofa; sitting in the window with the sun pouring through the Venetian blinds. Every request is met with a, 'Da!'

As I'm replacing ink cartridges, my cell phone starts to vibrate and then begins to ring, quietly at first, building to a crescendo, like a coma patient regaining consciousness after 7 years dreaming he was about to open a door. Only this time the door opens onto the stage during the last night of the Proms;

'And did those feet in ancient times,
Walk upon England's mountains green?
And was the Holy Lamb of God
On England's pleasant pastures seen?'
I flip open the phone, 'Bring me my bow of burning gold!'
'Dave?'
'Bring me my arrows of desire!'
'Talk to me Dave!'
'Bring me my...Ms Metro!' I say, 'Yo!'
'Caught in the moment?'
'That's who I am,' I say.

'Anyway, as requested, there's two tickets awaiting for you at the Royal Academy courtesy of Metro, and Alan says bell him, he has an idea for a project. Incidentally how's it going with the Russian babe?'

'Cultural relations are good, we find we have much in common,' I say.

'I bet you do. She'll probably figure strongly in your show?'

'I figure, her figure will certainly figure in the exhibition, figuratively speaking...'

'Dave!' Says Ivanka, 'I am showered and ready for RA. We go now, Da?'

'Gotta go,' I say to Ms Metro.

25 minutes later we pull up outside the Royal Academy in Piccadilly and stroll through the courtyard past a huge stainless steel sculpture, reflecting, absorbing and standing impassive like a giant alien flower that has appeared in a beam of blinding light to confront us with mysteries of the universe...

'Dave!'

Ivanka breaks the spell of my pretentious reverie that Jeff Koons inspires.

'Dave, we arrive in the knickers of time, Da?'

??? 'I believe you mean, 'In the nick of time."

'Niet Dave. I am not wearing knickers this time.'

???!

'I leave my thong under your pillow so I can reclaim them later. I put them on. You spank them off, Da?'

At that moment a RA attendant approaches us, 'Comrade Ivanka?'

'Da.'

'I have priority tickets for you and a guest.'

'Spasiba, comrade custodian, I salute you and your red shirt, it reminds me of...'

'Your well spanked ass,' I say.

'You are right Dave. Da. But also reminds me of Mother Russia. We go in now? We have art to view.'

Ivanka, pausing only to touch up her lipstick, slowly saunters up the steps to the exhibition. I follow behind, better to appreciate the latex covered bum swaying to its own erotic rhythm, and listening to the staccato sound of 8" stilettos striking the wooden floors.

We become hot topic of conversation amongst the Friday afternoon audience of day trippers, sherry swiggers and parish vicars up for the afternoon of art porn to fuel their 20 minutes of release at an address in Paddington on the way back to the Underground.

'Who's she?'

'Isn't that what's his name. Paints nude women for a living.'

'Is that his girlfriend?'

'She must be a model.'

'Latex.'

'Linen.'

'I'm going on a diet!'

'I'm not a lesbian but I'd sleep with both of them.'

'Why didn't they pick my picture?'

There is a startling cry of 'Dave!' Ivanka is standing before a large oil painting on wood panels depicting an erotic scene of curvaceous women on stage.

'They could be me Dave, I could be them. I am so hot! Who is this magnificent artist? What is this piece called?'

'The artist is Allen Jones, a master of the nude. What it's called? I dunno.'

Ivanka shouts across the gallery, 'Comrade Custodian! Yes you in the colours of Mother Russia. I need help da!'

The gallery attendant walks over, gesturing, with his finger to his lips for quiet. 'What can I do for you miss?'

'The name of this magnificent painting?'

The attendant takes out of his pocket a paperback List of Works, flicks to the relevant page and says, 'It's called Razzle-Dazzle.'

'By Stalin's mustache! Take me home now Dave. I am in need of razzle dazzle over the sofa! Comrade Custodian call us cab, da?'

The attendant, placing the List of Works over his erection, says, 'but you haven't seen the other Jones' piece!'

'By Lenin's goatee, there is more? Take us to it, da?'

Walking through gallery after gallery at quite a pace, we receive polite applause from visitors thinking we're a performance piece. We reach the Lecture Room gallery. On the wall before us is a brilliantly executed life size sculptural piece. Made of painted glass and reinforced plastic it involves a nubile woman, wearing a pink bodysuit, nestling in what appears to be crumpled tissue paper. The work is titled 'Think Pink.'

Ivanka stares, sweat beading her top lip, 'I think I cannot stand the power of this work. This artist knows how to paint strong women. It is shining example of Western decadence; it is erotically sublime. It is coldly executed but observationally it exudes a powerful eroticism. Trotsky would tut. I on the other hand am inflamed. Take me to your studio now, your sofa is waiting for us.'

'Comrade Custodian,' I say, handing him a perfectly folded £20 note, 'escort us to the taxi rank.'

Ivanka flew Aeroflot out of Heathrow to Moscow at 10.55am the next day, promising to be back for the opening night of my exhibition. The pressure was on me to get a move on and create some work.

There was only one thing to do.

I climbed through the bathroom window and telephoned Alan...

Excerpts from an Artist's (so-called) life...

INTERLUDE

The Horror! The Horror!

'Well Dave, could you tell us about a few of your favourite things?'
'I'm glad you asked, Rufus. Glad you asked.'

Attack of the Fifty-Foot Woman.
Dracula. Dr Jekyll + Mr Hyde..
Frankenstein. Freddy Krueger.
Godzilla. Jason Voorhees.
King Kong. Michael Myers.
M. Phantom of the Opera.
The Cabinet of Dr Caligari.
The Fly. The Invisible Man.
The Hunchback of Notre Dame.
The Incredible Shrinking Man.
The Mummy. The Nightmare before Christmas.
The Rocky Horror Picture Show.
The Shining. The Thing. The Wolfman.

'All of these should be sourced in their original versions, except The Thing, only the John Carpenter remake will do.'
'Thank you.'
'No Rufus, thank you.'

www.ingramcontent.com/pod-product-compliance
Lightning Source LLC
Chambersburg PA
CBHW070905180526
45168CB00005B/1932